AS I HEAR THE RAIN

PEN AMERICA
2019 PRISON WRITING AWARDS ANTHOLOGY

Published by: PEN America

Book Design by: Robert Pollock, Anjali Emsellem

Cover Image by: Tamara Santibañez

Cover Design by: Caits Meissner and Robert Pollock

Typefaces: Book Antiqua, Neutraface Text, Have Heart Two

ISBN: 9781686653490

Notes

The Honorable Mention prose and drama pieces appear in these pages as excerpts. All the work featured in this anthology, along with the author biographies, can be read in full on PEN America's website by visiting the Prison Writing Contest archive at pen.org/prison-writing.

The original essays *Parole Reform* and *Mass Incarceration:the Shame of a Nation* feature MLA-style references not included in this book. You can find the pieces in their intended format at pen.org/prison-writing.

Founded in 1971, the PEN America Prison Writing Program believes in the restorative, rehabilitative and transformative possibilities of writing. We provide hundreds of imprisoned writers across the country with free writing resources, skilled mentors, and audiences for their work.

The Prison Writing Contest Prizes are sponsored by the generous support of the Greenburger Center for Social & Criminal Justice.

We are thrilled to share that the newly named PEN America/Edward Bunker Prize in Fiction has been made possible by the legacy of Edward Bunker and the gift of his family. Learn more about Edward Bunker in the opening to the fiction chapter in this book.

Additionally, we are excited that the family of Madeleine L'Engle, an early mentor in our PEN America Prison Writing Program, has sponsored the institution of a new annual award: The L'Engel-Rahman Prize for Mentorship, which, beginning in 2020, will recognize three outstanding mentors in our program. This support will enable us to honor the memory and inspiration of Madeleine L'Engle's extraordinary connection with Ahmad Rahman through PEN America's program of awards and mentoring for incarcerated writers. PEN America's Prison Writing Program is made possible in part by the above donors, as well as generous funding from the Stavros Niarchos Foundation, Heising Simons Foundation, the Present Progressive Fund, and Catapult/New Balloon.

Illustration by Tamara Santibañez

About the Art

When soliciting artists for this anthology, we turned to an incredible project from Tamara Santibañez of Discipline Press: *When You're Gone*, a DIY-style stationary set assembled from photocopied black and white pencil drawings, all by incarcerated artists. Each piece also includes the artist's contact information, an invitation to participate in creative exchange through the walls. The artists featured in this book were discovered in *When You're Gone*'s pages, and directly commissioned to visually respond to our award-winning author's work. Celebrating Tamara's vision, we asked her to create an image for our cover art, which she graciously donated, and invited her to expound on the project that directly inspired this anthology's visuals.

— Caits Meissner
PEN America Prison and Justice Writing Program Director

A message from Tamara Santibañez:

Mail exchanges have always held a kind of magic to me. As a young person in the pre-internet age, the mail was often the only way to access precious cassette tapes, t-shirts, zines, and information. Sometimes the only way to request something was to send something else in exchange. One small point of access could lead to a world of knowledge that otherwise felt so far away, and bring it in just a little bit closer.

In encountering the prison system's communication restrictions, I am reminded of that time in my life. There are countless differences between the two exchanges, but the multitudes of hope that an envelope can contain remain the same. That any amount of hope can make it through a complex net of censorship, mailroom restrictions, contraband regulations, and stretches of segregation and solitary confinement is a miracle. That it is not only hope, but courageous works of creativity, authorship, political ideology, imagination, and compassion that make their way across the prison walls is a stunning testament to the human spirit.

When I attended Black & Pink's exhibit of work by incarcerated LGBTQIA+ artists at Abrons Art Center a few years back, I was not only struck by the artwork itself, but by the system they had created to text a message to a code. The message would then be converted to a letter, which would be sent to the individual artist as a way for the audience to connect. My own pen pal relationships with artists on the inside have been an unending source of strength and inspiration. In compiling the When You're Gone stationery set, I hoped to give others a sense of how mutually rewarding communicating with artists on the inside can be, as well as to showcase the artwork in a more intimate medium that could continue the magic of the mail.

— Tamara Santibañez
Discipline Press

Contents

ILLUSTRATIONS

I hope my work is received the same way that they would receive their peers in the literary community. Not as something less than or something marginalized, but as something equal, or something striving to be equal... All writers share a similar internal landscape that we visit, maybe fall asleep under a weeping willow, muse in a clover field, breath vitality from the breeze that loves us enough to caress our face with cool hand. All I ask from the outside literary community is to read and listen to my/our work with complete mindfulness and openness. You never know when we will meet each other on that same internal landscape.

— B. Batchelor
2011-2017 Multi-Prize winner in Poetry,
PEN America Prison Writing Awards

Introduction

CAITS MEISSNER

In October of 2018, through the generosity of the Minnesota Prison Writers Workshop, I had the opportunity to sit in person, at a number of different facilities, with a handful of writers who'd won awards in the PEN America Prison Writing Contest. New to the organization, I was keen to learn the legacy of the program I'd inherited, specifically as interpreted by the people we work with. Through these meetings I began to understand the profound opportunity our program offers: a clear home for work written in prison that rigorous judging, and celebration of work written in prison. Many incarcerated writers describe the sense of validation the awards provide for their path, and the creation of a literary connection and presence that extends beyond prison walls. And it is no small achievement to be awarded. The winning work in this anthology was chosen from over *one thousand* entries.

But—and there was always a but—most of the writers we work with closely have also shared that they don't really want to be seen as a "prison writer." What is a prison writer, anyway?

Jevon Jackson, first place poetry winner in this year's contest wrote, "My hopes for how my work is received by the literary community outside is that it connects simply to the point where it is not passively embraced as work from an 'imprisoned writer', but from a Writer who writes about his pain, his imprisonment, his joy, his relationships, his life. My hope is also that the literary community out there can see themselves in some aspect of my shared experience."

We operate with the knowledge that for writers in prison, access to participation in the literary community is severely limited by layers of walls, both literal and metaphorical. As literary advocates grappling with the ethics of writing in an era of mass incarceration, the well intentioned among us (including ourselves) often unintentionally replicate the suppression and isolation of the very system we seek to challenge. Our anthology is a kind of wonderful paradox. We are both so terrifically proud to both feature excellent writing, and use the platform to disrupt limiting ideas about who is in prison, and what they are capable of. But our efforts stretch further. We'd like all of the writers in this anthology to also place their work in other venues, ones that are not reserved only for those incarcerated. And thus, in the past year, our work in the PEN America Prison and Justice Writing Program has moved with intention toward reintegrating exiled voices into our broader literary worlds. We began to ask: How do we begin to un-silo the writer in prison from the flattening "prison writer" label? How can we bring voices from behind the walls into authentic relationship with our existing communities?

Walking towards these questions, the release of our 2nd annual PEN America Prison Writing Anthology coincides with a series of events titled BREAK OUT, a movement to (re)integrate incarcerated writers into literary community. In order to accomplish this, we have invited New York City-based reading series to offer a featured writer slot to an incarcerated writer during the month of September through a stand-in reader or an audio recording. Most local reading series have a mix of loyal attendees and rotating newcomers who come to see the advertised featured reader. Instead of always asking the community to attend prison writing events—which often attract those who are already curious about the conversation on mass incarceration—we are bringing incarcerated writers into already established literary community, featured alongside outside writers as colleagues and equal contributors. We are proud to report that over 2 dozen reading series have signed on to this boundary-pushing project to feature an incarcerated writer during the month. Our friends at The Poetry Project have additionally helped us to secure a handful of venues across the United States.

As a PEN America team of two, we are keenly aware that the needs of the writers we work with outsize our resources. But our hope is for our event series to be a conversation starter, with the goal of extending the effort far beyond September's bounds. In preparation, this August we gathered participating reading series curators for a community conversation about the framing, ethics, and presentation of the work, and called on the attendees to help create a future vision of radical literary inclusion. Understanding the importance of hearing from the writers themselves, we invited a handful of our featured writers to share what they want the literary community to know about their experience, desires and ideas for inclusion.

"My hope," Spoon Jackson wrote in response, "is that the literary community know they have fellow writers incarcerated who would welcome their exchange with letters and critique—I mean there is so much, so many depths an incarcerated writer can bring to the outside literary community that will enhance their writing, and it can be a two-way street. There are such intense and to-the-bone experiences that can be shared with outside writing communities, and art and writing suffers without fellowship."

We agree. In hopes of facilitating this exchange, readers of this anthology are welcome to share feedback to the writer's featured in this anthology by emailing us at prisonwriting@pen.org. Additional answers from the questions we posed are featured throughout the anthology as quotes, and gathered in the back of the book.

Synchronisitically, this is also the year that we announce our fiction prize in the Prison Writing Awards has now been officially named the PEN America/Edward Bunker Prize in Fiction, thanks to a generous underwriting from his family. Bunker's legacy bridges these very inside/outside divides, creating an aspirational tale of almost mythical proportions. While Bunker never forgot, or wrote away, his history—in fact, he leaned into his nearly two decade prison past—he also found himself in a rare dream: his best-selling novels became movies starring Hollywood heavyweights such as Dustin Hoffman and John Voight. I invite you to read more about Edward Bunker's extraordinary story at the start of the fiction chapter.

May this anthology serve a multitude of purposes: may it introduce new readers to exceptional works, may vividly depicted shared experiences speak to the other writers in this book, may the work inform those without relationship to anyone held in United States prisons, may a reader forget the work was written from prison, altogether. May this book inspire literary communities to more intentionally include the work of incarcerated writers, and may it lead to new paths for both writers and readers alike.

Congratulations to all of our winners, and congrats to you, reader. You're holding a vault full of gems in your hand. When a facet of truth or beauty catches your eye in these pages, you are encouraged to turn it over, examine it, and share it. Everyone deserves a bit of this shine.

With gratitude,

Caits Meissner
PEN America Prison and Justice Writing Program Director

Bright lights, big city. I aspire to fame inasmuch as most people do. Who in their life has not entertained a daydream of being a high-profile artist? I want to someday do an interview on Fresh Air, and be featured on a segment of the PBS Newshour. Such things, however, do not occur without people, That is, if no one hears or sees my work, the work will remain confined to the limits of my existence. Of course, I had better put together damn good work if I want recognition.

I want notoriety and acclaim within the literary community because I have this dream that if my work becomes significant enough it will help me get out of prison—be it commutation, or parole, or whatever. Is that realistic, or does it fall within the theme of David Hammons' "Higher Goals" sculpture? At the same time anything I achieve affects the collective. With a spotlight, prison and the issues of mass incarceration appear in the background. Any level of fame I gain also gives me a platform to highlight prison issues.

— Sean J. White
2014-2017, Multi-Prize winner in Poetry and Drama,
PEN America Prison Writing Awards

2019 PEN AMERICA/EDWARD BUNKER PRISON WRITING AWARDS IN **FICTION**

INTRODUCING THE NEWLY NAMED
PEN AMERICA/EDWARD BUNKER PRIZE IN FICTION

At an event held in May 2019, PEN America celebrated the naming of the Edward Bunker Prize in Fiction by hosting a preview reading of our 2019 Prison Writing Fiction Award winners, capped with a panel exploring Edward's legacy. A longtime friend, actor Danny Trejo, recalled his days on the set of *Runaway Train*, where Trejo has been hired as a drug counselor to keep a featured actor clean. When somebody asked him to be an extra in the film, Trejo asked, "Extra what?"

"Can you act like a convict? The man asked.

"And," Trejo continued, "I thought about my past: Soledad prison, San Quentin, Folsom, Susanville, Vacaville and I said, `I'll give it a shot.'"

Edward—or Eddie, as friends called him—who was one of *Runaway Train*'s screenwriters, remembered Trejo from his days winning boxing matches at San Quentin prison, where Eddie has previously served as the captain's clerk. They started catching up.

"They're gonna give me $50 for acting like a convict," Trejo said, sharing with our audience, "and we both kinda laughed because we'd been doing it for free for a long time."

Eddie offered Trejo his first job teaching an actor to box for $320 a day, and the rest was history—Trejo was ushered into Hollywood, and Eddie became Trejo's mentor. Aside from helping Trejo understand how to work successfully on a movie set, Eddie offered sage advice in humility, "The whole world can think you're a movie star, but you can't."

Danny Trejo's humorous story offers just a small glimpse of writer, screenwriter and actor Edward Bunker's extraordinary legacy, which grew from humble beginnings. Like many of the writers who reach out to the PEN America Prison and Justice Writing Program, Eddie was involved with the justice system for decades before finding significant success as an author. In fact, his writing career began while incarcerated, typing on the same prison-sanctioned Swintec clear-plastic typewriter that our award-winning writers still use today. In 1973, after 17 years of trial and error, Eddie finally landed a deal from behind the walls when *No Beast So Fierce*, a novel about a paroled man struggling with the reentry process, was published as his literary debut.

I sat on the littlest toilet at the rear of the cell, shining the hideous bulb-toed shoes that were issued to those being released. Through my mind ran an exultant chant - I'll be a free man in the morning. But for all the exultation, the joy of leaving after eight calendars in prison was not unalloyed. My goal in buffing the Adley shoes was not so much to improve their appearance as to relieve tension. I was more nervous in facing release on parole than I had been on entering so long ago.

It helped slightly to know that such apprehensiveness was common, though often denied, by men to whom the world outside was increasingly vague as the years passed away. Enough years in prison and a man would be as ill-equipped to handle the demands of freedom as a Trappist monk thrown into the maelstrom of New York City. At least the monk would have his faith to sustain him, while a former prisoner would possess memory of previous failure - of prison and the incandescent awareness of being a ex-convict, a social outcast.

(From Edward Bunker's No Beast So Fierce)

Five years later the book *No Beast So Fierce* became the movie Straight Time, starring Dustin Hoffman.

Eddie, as friends and family called him, went on to write numerous books—some of which have been adapted into major motion pictures featuring prominent actors such as Eric Roberts, Jon Voight, Steve Buscemi and others—and he was a screenwriter on *Straight Time* (1978), *Runaway Train* (1985) and *Animal Factory* (2000). He also appears on screen as an actor in a number of films, most famously as Mr. Blue in *Reservoir Dogs*.

On the May 2019 panel, Eddie's wife, Jennifer Steele, spoke about his perserverance: "He was in prison without a mother or father or anyone else outside," she said. "He sold his blood to get his papers outside and to get his work published. He had this incredible reach and drive to make something good and lasting come out of these incredible circumstances."

Of course, Eddie was a crime writer, and combed his own dramatic life experience to propel his realistically rendered stories. A New York Times article quoted Eddie, who said in an interview, "It has always been as if I carry chaos with me the way others carry typhoid. My purpose in writing is to transcend my existence by illuminating it." We see that very energy, drive and purpose in so many of our own writers who win the Prison Writing Awards.

The PEN America/Edward Bunker Prison Writing Prize in Fiction is a profound addition to our long history of work with and advocacy on behalf of incarcerated writers, and we are deeply grateful to the family of Edward Bunker for supporting the PEN America Prison and Justice Writing Program. Brendan, Eddie's son, shared with our audience during the panel, "I know he's really happy, looking down on us."

We like to think so, too.

First Prize, Fiction

First World Problems
KEVIN SCHAEFFER

Monday, March 9th

Better take a seat, Future Self, or have you remembered? Farley died
last night. That obnoxious clown, Shots Fired, is banging on his door at
some absurd hour hollering down the tier: "You're too late, coppers!
He dead now!" I'm miffed, sure, but groggy enough to roll over and
knock back out. I have this crazy, sort of deep-sleep claustrophobic
nightmare when I'm back under, too — I know, we agreed on no more
dream entries unless they're especially raunchy, but I think you'll find
this one... let's say, revelatory. I'm on the floor, all crumpled up, and
my spirit or whatever raises up out of my body. There I am: a scrawny
little shit, looking more worn down than any twenty-something should.
And spirit-me starts darting all over the place. Never felt so boxed
in before, this sudden, overwhelming need for open space. So I ram
against the thin slits of window: impassable. Hurtle across the cell and
ram against the door. Try to push under, but there's all that rolled-up
newspaper stuffed there to muffle the block noise. Swoosh up to the
vents, but they're all taped up with cardboard — it's still March here,

on my end, and the heat's been at full-blast. I'm floating, scrambling. Sheer desperation sets in. So I dive into the porcelain basin of the sink, push with all my strength until I've squeezed through the tiny drain holes, and then I'm winding down through miles of plumbing, zooming, gaining momentum, bliss, whatever, until I finally burst out into nothingness.

Wake up for count drenched in sweat. Toilet won't flush when I take my morning piss. No water in the pipes either. Maintenance? At this hour? Orlin's fuming, rattling the sink buttons and going on about all the indignities he's suffered in his life. We can both get testy without our coffee, sure, but Orlin's on another level. Persecution complex flares up. And to make things worse, he ran out of rolling papers yesterday. Ask him what all that fuss was about last night, but he's too riled: "Is it too much, as a human being, to get some hot flipping water around here, or haven't these people heard of a little document called the Constitution of America?!"

Chow runs late, when we're finally heading out, and I see the police tape all over Farley's door, one of the bottom tier single cells. Nothing registers. I mean, he wasn't even in there — gone for almost a week now, up on observation or something. (Unless they would have brought him back after count last night?) Was it... last Saturday I'd seen him last? He'd been all ready to stay up for some blaxploitation double feature on TCM Underground, never went to dinner, or breakfast the next day. Figured it was some medical thing, but no one really knew — they were all asking me. "What, you don't know?" They'd all gawked, incredulous. And sure, F.S., he was basically my... best friend? But only best prison friend. You know, nothing too personal, nothing too deep. Don't even know what he's in for. Never came up. Mostly, we walked to chow together. Light stuff. Banter. And... well, so what if he was my only friend, besides? Who's even counting? You?

Get caught in the current along the walk to chow, everyone full of speculation about him and the water situation (apparently the whole block's dry). Up ahead, Shots is setting the scene for all in earshot: the startled demeanor of the bumbling night C.O. as he passed Farley's door on rounds, the 20 min lapse before Medical strolled briskly — but not too briskly — onto the block, Farley's body pulled limply into the open. Blood everywhere. Someone pipes: "Sarge told me he cut a hole so big you could fit your whole fist inside," before I consciously zone them all out. It's all just action to them, a blip in the routine of an otherwise ho-hum prison day. And anyway, by the time we clear Education and the chapel, turn up toward the chow hall, they all shut up, slow to a stand still: the powder-blue water tower capped with snow on the wooded hill past G-Block, the one that looms over us every day stamped "BENTHAM" in case we ever forget for one freaking second where we all are — that tower's unleashing a steady white spray from its belly.

Post- breakfast, the announcement bigres across the prison: "The institution is currently under a partial state of emergency. Water usage is hereby suspended. This is not a drill." A slow trickle of updates all morning: we're semi-locked down, in a sort of confinement limbo. No classes or programs or activities. No yard or block-out. Most workers won't report. No visits, no mail. Stay tuned regarding access to basic hydration and sanitation needs. This all really gears Orlin up. He would've made a fine proletarian cog about a hundred years ago, primed to wade mindlessly into some subversive fray. After this, his second rant of the day, he rolls a cigarette with a page from the back of his pocket New Testament — "Its okay," he justifies, pointing to heaven. "I know how it all ends" — and gets started on his lame fantasy drawings for the day. Meanwhile, I'm keeping tabs on Farley's door all morning. Maybe someone else get moved in there yesterday and I missed it? Farley could still be up in Medical, or the Hole, or wherever he'd been. Rumors are wrong here all the time — why not this one?

Around 9am, D---- yells over the block P.A. that water would be turned back on for like 5 mins. "Fill your mugs and drop your dumps," he advises. "Or forever hold 'em." What follows is a truly groan-worthy slapstick routine of Orlin and I rushing about the cell, gathering our mugs and bowls and random plastic bags and containers, even my dirty washtub (about 11 qts) — the water cold, and at low pressure, taking precious minutes to fill, and these various receptacles proving challenging (for Orlin at least) to stack and store, water sloshing all over the floor and rugs, bags tipping over or slipping out of hands in transit, our clothes soaked. Then, as I'm more properly tying off bags at the desk, Orlin hangs the curtain. After a silent minute, I tell him to hurry, that I have needs too, but he just gets almost shrill with exasperation — "Don't talk to me on the toilet!" and wastes the last ninety seconds, grunting and straining away.

Some simple figures, F.S.: Bentham houses approx. 2,200 men, split into East and West sides. Assume about 250 per block, with five blocks on the West Side, that's +/- 1,250. At some point this afternoon, they set up a bank of porta-potties in the zone leading to the yard. A whopping 14, I hear, on either side. 14 into 1,250 = 89 men per toilet. So: if they start running toilets immediately following 1pm count all the way until 9 pm count (with a 30 min interlude for 4 pm count, and assuming they run optimally, to the last second before these counts, and movement is never otherwise halted, and staff is capable of running them optimally, free if resentment or incompetence, and each of these 89 selflessly takes only the time due to them; and that no one will require more than one visit within the allotted period), how long can each of these 89 adult men indulge for their personal relief of the day?

(*Answer = barely 5 mins.*)

How to describe this odd day? There's an uneasiness about it. Something's off. I try working in the new story, but my notes are such a mess and don't have the focus to organize them. I try to put a dent in 2666, but nothing clicks. I know, F.S., greatness won't come from shirking our studies, but what can be done? At both lunch and dinner, I find myself instinctively waiting around for Farley, half-expecting him to stride through the tape, all smiles, some snarky comment at the ready. For years, I'd walked to chow alone. Didn't mind. As an only child, I'm tempered to a certain degree of loneliness. But now, back on my own for the past week after years of walking with Farley, can't help but feel this all to be some relapse, an unhealthy regression into myself. We'd known each other... three years? Maybe doesn't sound like much, F.S., but that's, what... almost 3,300 meals, 3,300 conversations? Minimum. How many does it take to feel like you finally know someone — to trust? How many books or memories or petty prison policies discussed before you develop a dependence on him? By dinner, we're all just making a quick trip up and back anyway. Everything's in styrofoam. And people are so revved and wide-eyed by this point, from the novelty of the day, from the hazy implications of a waterless future, that Farley stops coming up in small talk. Old news, I guess. Or short attention spans.

Don't even touch the icy, flesh-toned poultry patty. Just lie around all night, watching Pickpocket and most of A Man Escaped, ignoring Orlin's bellyaching over the subtitles. Usually enjoy the cool repetition of Bresson, the sensitive and over-trusting characters trounced by an unforgiving world, but I'm too distracted today. Maybe I'm getting a cold — or is that just the caffeine withdrawal? By count, it's obvious our block is burnt on the porta-potties until tomorrow. I wait until I'm sure Orlin's asleep, then hang the curtain and squat over an empty chip bag. It will still be warm in the morning.

Still Monday

A late-night insight (written by book lamp): To be clear — this is NOT denial. But before I go through the stress and anguish of processing all this — Farley, everything — I'm wondering... do I even need to? I mean, prison friendships are by their very nature fugitive, perishable. People disappear here all the time. Without warning. By night or broad daylight. Transferred. Hole-hauled. Released. Or just moved to the opposite side of the prison — a mere 200 yards away, which might as well be Mongolia. Maybe never to be seen again. Or best-case scenario, one or both of us get paroled someday: contact and congregation forbidden. All relationships here are a gamble, investing that most precious of resources: emotional energy. You hatch into a social butterfly yet, F.S.? Have you got the game all figured out? I don't know how people do it here, putting themselves out there with all that risk of loss. Doesn't it hurt them? Isn't it so much easier to stay curled up? Faced inward? And sure, part of me will always be grateful to Farley for lugging me out of that grim, years-long seclusion, but just thinking if, all things considered, it's not just best and easiest, for my own mental well-being and all, to imagine he's... well, released and free's a bit too sugary. But moved, maybe? Transferred to be closer to his family? Right. So he moved. He's good. We're all good, then.

Tuesday, March 10th

Wake up feeling... empty. Glum. Is this what loss feels like, F.S.? Who else have you mourned by now, or did you never weather this one? Have I been writing a figment? Is the future nothing but dry, barren wastes? Parched earth, unpopulated?

Already groggy from the get-go; starting Day Two without that essential coffee bump. Don't drink it like some of these fiends around here, guzzling entire 4 oz. bags in 2-3 days, but still need it to unmuddle my mushy morning brain. Orlin's starting to smell. Everything is, really. We've been using the cell toilet for #1's, covering it up with one of my old shirts. They finally call us for porta-potties after breakfast — our first opportunity. More were added overnight, up to maybe 40 now. I'll spare you the math; it's just chaos on a grander scale. Freezing out, too. Maybe mid-thirties? Huge lines stuck waiting, no organization. Must have called three blocks at once. And most don't have their coats either, I'm guessing to make stuffing into the porta-potties a more manageable prospect. So everyone's shivery, uncaffeinated and extra-irritable. To think just two weeks ago we were in full blizzard mode here. Still a ton of snow around too — 2 or 3 feet, with 4 foot banks along the walk from shovelings. Imagine the impact of one last wintry attack at this moment of vulnerability: a true shitstorm.

Anyway, as I'm waiting, one of those holier-than Kooks is rattling off scripture to a rapt disciple: "This has all happened before, you realize, Water into Blood? The Weeping Tower, Brother Farley's untimely demise — what might we glean from such happenings? Perhaps they are but the first in a series of plagues wrought to sway the Commonwealth into freeing its ill-treated inmate masses from captivity." Pinch us, F.S.

No one's really locking in on the block anymore. They're all just sort of… lingering, in the dayroom, on the tiers, griping and commiserating, Laughtrack offering his inexhaustible cackle-commentary. A water cooler has been set up by the C.O.'s desk while I was out, but it's already dry. No rationing. Great. Especially since Orlin managed to topple most of our receptacles while dinking about in the night, we're down to my washtub, sitting uncovered since yesterday and infused with tart detergenty undertones. I catch the hazmat crew when they show up to clean Farley's cell. Rubber gloves, face masks, these thin plastic aprons. One of them carries in a 5 gallon jug for the cooler and dumps it, glug glug glug, into a mop bucket. They pull away the tape, set upon the blood. In there awhile, two — premium work, at 51¢ an hour. Dispatched for stabbings, D-Code shower craps, the occasional act of self-murder. Afterwards, Sarge carts up all his stuff. Footlocker of books and papers, laundry bags of faded sweats and sneakers, a records box of food, that shitty, over-priced flat screen. Could his family really sift through such things, stricken with grief, and think: "Our son?" Reminds me: he still had my copies of Notes from Underground and Boethius. And I still have his Las Casas. For a second, I even wonder: did he leave me something — a note? Would they let me have it if he did?

Just can't seem to focus on this damn story. Voice is the main problem — it all just ends up sounding like me. And Bolaño's too dense right now. The whole routine's just gonna have to wait until things are back to normal. Sorry, posterity. Since everything's cancelled again, figure I'll dig out some old journals and see how our rosy pal YesterSelf saw things. Oldest entry I can find on Farley is from the Fall of 2012:

"Eat chow with this guy Macilwraith again today, Seems alright, We've just been sort of falling in with each other on the walks up for the past few days. Now, don't get ahead of yourself, F.S. We're not best buds or anything. But have been thinking about this more, ever since reading that self-help book from the library, Solitudinarians Anonymous, and that one exercise. Er... Actually wasn't gonna tell you about it, but there was this one graphic of some chiseled guy on a desert island called "No Man is an Island" with these little blanks that were supposed to be bridges I guess, and you were supposed to fill in the names of your support system to show yourself how you're not really as isolated as you think, or something. Well, I sat for hours with it and... Nevermind. can't get too emotional (Lusk's in the cell right now.) Point is one friend couldn't hurt, right?"

Here's one of my favorites, from about two years ago (July 2013):

"Well, F.S., Farley's officially got himself an arch nemesis: C.O.N----- . Remember how there's this dress code policy where you always need your brown state shirt on when you're off the block, even when wearing a jacket that's buttoned all the way, and the shirt's not visible? If a tree falls in the woods, and all that? Well, N----- starts pulling aside Farley on our walls to chow, cause Farley always wears his jacket buttoned, and N------'s a real stickler for that stuff and always demands to see a shirt collar or else he'll burn him for chow. So now, every day before we head up there, Farley'll triple-check himself in the mirror, make sure his collar's totally tucked in under his jacket, so N----'ll pull him over and be denied the satisfaction of a petty bust. His disappointment each time is truly palpable. This might be the single most perfect expression of civil disobedience I've ever witnessed."

Find more than I expected. Seeing him and the other Native Service guys at Drum Circle practice outside the chapel on Monday mornings as

I went to pick up commissary, all of them chanting and pounding away. That time he brought me a little bundle of venison from their annual feast. Tons of zingers and book recs. Among all these crinkly pages, I find him. Broken into cubist-like fragments. A graph of subtly shifting moods and prison wear. And yet there's nothing... to make sense of all this. He knew so many people, was personable in a sarcastic, almost dickish way. Was practically... spitefully defiant. The type who'd grow out his religiously-exempt hair only to snub shoulder-length restrictions. Who'd max out a sentence just to bleed the state of resources. It's hard to see his death as anything but a defeat. For him and for all of us. I've been struggling to exorcise these clichés from my brain all afternoon, questions I don't really want to ask myself: what did I miss? Could I have done something more? I mean, I talked to the guy every single day — was I blind?

Guess it's to be expected, but keep thinking of our own stretch way back in county. Suddenly stalled with that unbearable guilt, the sense of a shrunken world, shame of stripped rights and squandered life. Onset of the Dark Time's basically inevitable. Mistake was confiding to the counselor. "I'm feeling... I don't know. Sad. And empty. Sad and empty all the time." "Are you thinking of hurting yourself or others?" "...No?" Tossed in an observation tank for over a week — 10 days, wasn't it? — just a mattress and a turtle suit and all those dark thoughts swirling around. Poisoning me. Well, lesson learned: help was no help at all. They just wanted to cover their asses, scribble down all your faults in their Big Book to hold against you later. So stay out of sight, keep your problems to yourself. Maybe things will get tolerable someday. On that last day, a voice through the food-slot: "Feeling better now?" Almost delirious: "Oh yes, so much better! Thank you!" Can't imagine what pushed Farley to that point. A loss of his own? An illness? Just that crushing recognition that there's nothing left for you in this day-in-day-out slog? It hurts to think of him locked away up there all last week, severed from contact with family and friends, deprived of prison's few luxuries; mulling over whatever wrong words or actions that had brought him to such a dead end, and comforted only by the vindictive thought: just let me out of here for one day, you bastards, one minute, and you'll never have power over me again..

I expect no answers, No closure. I just hope it was fast.

Slop again. Portions always get smaller, less edible for lockdowns. It's the styrofoam effect. Everything jumbled about inside, packaged hours in advance. Congealed soy paste and rice, Jell-O, soggy bread. On the walk back, this guy Cray falls in with me. Him and Farley used to play chess on the block all the time. "Man, that's something about Farley." "Yea," I choke. (Get it together.) "Gotta admit, had me tearing up a bit earlier. He was a good dude." With a side glance, I check to see if he's being genuine. Seems it, but people are so hard to read here. Honestly catches me off guard that I'm not the only person dealing with this — in a flash, I imagine a friendship with this person, taking up Farley's former seat, besting him with variations of the Sicilian Defense and back-rank mates. But I'm silent, squash the idea. "Well, be easy," he says, and moves on. Where did this big knot in my gut come from? Seems like the water's spraying out on the tower even faster than yesterday, so much waste. Should I call home today? Could that help? It's been… a long time. Trays are tossed all along the banks of snow. And world's so out of whack wouldn't surprise me to see flicking across the wall a bunch of these tiny frogs that show up in springtime. "They will come up into your palace and your bedroom and onto your bed, into the houses of your officials and on your people…" Multitudes tunneling out of the snow, smooshed onto the cement in rough outlines of state boot heels. Yea, think I need a nap or something..

Back in the cell, Orlin's made a big mug of cold instant coffee. Chugging it down, his face says it all: do not make my mistakes. I sit at the desk, picking at my food and watching the local news. For a whole thirty seconds, they cover "the death of an inmate at SCI-Bentham." Farley Macilwraith, aged 38, serving 30 years for armed robbery and aggravated assault. I give up on the rice. "Found unresponsive late Sunday night, State Police investigating." No reference to suicide (or the prison-wide water crisis; for that matter). No personal details at all. Defined for the public, one last time, only by his worst self. I never even knew how old he was, F.S. Gist of this coverage has to be the bleakest thing all day. At ease, folks. Justice has been served. Someone, somewhere, was celebrating.

No more heavy thinking today, Please No TCM, no PBS docs—I let Orlin run the remote. We watch Deep Sea Detox and My Face is Not My Face! and Millennial Matchmaker: Miami-Dade. Finally get the allure of this "reality" stuff: it's deadening, almost narcotic. Makes you think you're not actually missing all that much out there. Go to bed expecting Farley to visit me in a dream, the price of all today's wallowing and reminiscing—I'm thinking some half-man with a wispy genie tail hovering over my bunk, absolving me of any responsibility toward him, "Do not brood on such matters, dear friend," he'd moan. "Leave me my problems, and worry of your own." But there's nothing, just surreal, drought-heavy impressions: scrabbling across polar wastes, clawing up the sides of an empty swimming pool, entombed in the dark of the tower's bone-dry hull. A long night. Restless.

Wednesday, March 11th

Everything reeks. I reek. Feel... subhuman. My skin's all scummy. Same with my face. Hair's greasy. Head might cleave open if I have to endure another day without coffee. When I focus on Orlin, I swear I can see a plume of gnats about his head and shoulders, zipping out his unbrushed mouth-hole, alighting in patchy beard growth. He's out of clean shirts already. No laundry running, obviously, but word is they'll be shipping some out to another prison at some point. How to describe this disgusting cell? There's food all over the place, caked on the desk, by the sink. This waft of piss, festering, seeping through the shirt-draped toilet. And sometime last night, Shots or Laughtrack blew our power trying to sting some ramen.

And the block? It's pure havoc. Lawless. All the unruliest bums and headcases permanently set up on the tiers, out in the dayroom. Never officially declared block-out, but I think the C.O.'s are worried people wouldn't listen if told to lock in. Defiance hangs heavy. Jungle calls and cries of "Anarchy!" Blasting stereos. Fire alarms constantly tripped from all the smoking in the cells. And the Administration hasn't seemed too concerned with improving the situation, either. Usually there's a white shirt or bigwig stopping by the block every few hours—but where are they now? Huddled in an office somewhere, dodging inquiries into the lack of oversight? Instead, condescending memos appear on the scrolling Powerpoint of the block channel, "Use this crisis as an opportunity to practice patience and responsibility." Talk about glass half-full. And then there's: "Hydration is happiness. Enjoy the tasty bottled water we've provided for you!" Except there are still zero attempts by D----- or anyone else to ration said water. Movement's been halted all morning from fights breaking out on different blocks over the shortages. Ultimately, I'm forced to stake out the cooler until they bring in the next jug from the storage closet or wherever. No wonder it's always dry—people hang about with big cereal bags and plastic tubs to take as much as they can carry. When Sarge finally brings the thing in, there's a mad rush, but I manage to fill our mugs. Back in the cell, Orlin takes his and clinks it against mine: "Absent friends!" Dude's driving me freaking bonkers, F.S. Has the attention span of a five-year old. One minute he's doodling some disproportionate and scantily-clad sorceress, the next tearing pictures of celebrities and bra ads out of magazines to hang in his lockers. And he's truly filthy, if I failed to mention. More tar than fingers at this point. He's chainsmoked right through Paul's epistles.

I hate the block, but need space. Spend half the day sulking in a corner. Flies everywhere. Gotta figure the place hasn't been cleaned since Friday now, and there's upwards of 500 styrofoams bagged up right out in the sallyport. The smells are... diverse. What's next? Disease? Boils? Something, something... should look that up later, prepare myself. I'm by this little cubby file of pamphlets on taboo prison issues—mental health, sexual assault, victim impact awareness. Thick film of dust over the bunch, probably all stuffed there years ago. There's one called Self-Termination — Maybe Not! Protecting Yourself or Loved Person from the Woeful Precipice. Wording's so awkward and stilted, I wonder if maybe it had been translated from some other language. A section inside reads: "Abiding Your Subjugated States: Have you lately undergone a loss of freedoms? Breakdown of personal intimacy-bond? Court of law proceeding and/or crime sentence conviction? All such things and more could inspire the attitude toward self-termination." The warning signs listed within really help raise my hackles:

Worthlessness, "scuttled hopes," agitation or aggressive posturing, anxiety, "withdrawal from wholesome interaction orbits," impulsiveness, pessimism, neglect of appearance, loss of control, fear or suspicion of others, lack of interests, sense of disconnection from self or surroundings, "desperation urges," edginess...

Like they asked someone to describe the average inmate — and yet it didn't capture Farley at all. Never saw anything close to self-destructive in him, beyond how he'd glaze every meal with salt. "Screw parole," he'd always kid. "I'm putting all my chips on the widowmaker." But there had to be something there, right? Hidden by shame, fear, even strength? Buried deep down within the person I knew?

It's that time. Have you grown tired yet, Future Self, of my detailing every gastric upheaval? Why this sudden, troubling fixation? Simple: this crisis has reduced me to some basic, animalistic foundation. Really, sub-animalistic. Animals can shit anywhere, anytime. Carefree. My needs occupy the entirety of my day, are at the mercy of inept overseers. Will they be met? What to do if they aren't? I'm fresh out of chip bags. And it's frustrating, sure. Even as a lowly inmate, my time and thoughts and energy could be so much better spent. Haven't touched our studies once today, for instance. There's at least 120 porta-potties on our side now, transforming the entire little zone leading to the yard into a sort of sanitation shanty town. Line creeps along, stalls while the outside workers pump out last night's dinner. People swap horror stories amid the wait, and sounds like the Special Needs Unit takes the cake. Apparently, some of the D-Codes over there still haven't comprehended that their toilets are out of order. Filled to the brim, as one man describes it. Another tells of an actual stench-aura that's encapsulated the entire outer structure of the block. Maybe in a bid to top all this grossness, the Universe sends out a couple kitchen workers, hands unwashed, on their way back to dietary to prep our next meal.

Movement. Up ahead, this guy in a wheelchair is struggling to transition into a porta-potty. "Let's go, Legs," from a supervising white shirt. "Gotta line here. And let's see that collar first... Okay." It's N----- of course, Farley's old foe. Lt. N----- now. Checking all those shirts got him a promotion, a hundred grand salary. My blood rises as I pass him. What a douche. Just since yesterday, the insides of the toilet have been completely covered with graffiti: "Kill All Ratz" and crudely-etched black hands, even one that says "FARLEY LIVES!" (Superstition: while I was on the block earlier, they moved some new dope into Farley's cell. Took less than 5 mins for Shots & Co. to fill him in on all the recent grisly horrors that went down inside, and the guy freaked, got himself hauled off to the ostensibly less-haunted cells of the Hole.) I'm all backed up. From outside, I hear N---- make a big show of yawning: "Almost quittin' time. Gonna go home and take a nice... long steam-m-my shower!" Pull the pen out my back pocket — why not? Along an open stretch by the door handle, my sole creative impulse of the day: "Lt. N----- eats throbbing convict dong."

Can just feel my fuse getting shorter all day. Appetite shrivels just from the walk to chow. Everyone's so nasty, ripe. And stupid. Spouting conspiracies about the tower. How it's all some elaborate govt. drill. A test. Or how the Superintendent owns a slice of the crapper company. Across the state, attorneys are being commissioned to draw up lawsuits. How could Farley abandon me to such dregs? Was my friendship worth so little? If he couldn't bear it, how the hell will I? Up ahead, in the chow line, bolted to the cinder blocks; I catch sight of some newly-hung poster—like, newly hung just since breakfast. Before I even read the thing, I process its sunrise imagery, my entire body is reeling with rage. Every part of me instinctively understands that this shitty, lamer mass-produced poster is the Administration's full and wanting response to Farley's death, and it pisses me the hell off. Luring the vulnerable toward the system's stern and inescapable tendrils. "Declare yourself," it might as well read, "so we can watch you more closely." Can't be mad at Farley for any of this. Just can't. When that darkness steals its way into your brain, twists and corrupts all logic, emotion, nothing seems to matter but stopping it. It's them I should be mad at. Capital "T" Them. The ones who studied away those dusty pamphlets instructing us to, "Retain vigilance. Report anomalous behavior of your friend or loved person to a certified treatment specialist forthwith." Put that weight on me, another depressed inmate faced with my own mound of messed-up shit, and boxed in besides by a puerile snitching code, to sell out my only friend, doom him to a deeper misery in observation, from where he'll be cut loose in a few days regardless. He was their responsibility. Their ward. And isn't this epidemic ages old by now? It's 2015, for Pete's sake! Dropping the ball with the water shit, okay. Benefit of the doubt, maybe they really weren't prepared for it. Need a little time to get their act together. But what's their excuse for Farley? All the pamphlets, the self-help books, they all say it's preventable—so what the hell are they waiting for?! "Hope is real." That's the full extent of bullshit on that bullshit poster. And you know, I bet it's a goddamn sunset.

Don't even remember the walk back. Don't have my tray with me either. I'm shaking. In the cell, Orlin's hand is on my shoulder: "Don't touch me, you filthy fuck!" "Whoa there, buddy. Easy, here, Paid Peñafort some of those girly clippings to sting us some water. Remember coffee?" Heat. Caffeine. God. "You, um... holding up alright, pardner?" Christ, F. S., when was the last time anyone's asked us that? When was the last time we've been shown a simple kindness? I'm too ashamed to respond. Just sit hunched at the desk, sipping my coffee like a weirdo, Orlin isn't so bad, as cellies go.

Snow: later in the day; some genius makes the connection that all this white stuff covering the compound is, essentially, water in another form. Orders trickle down to let us gather some up, for washing or diluting the cesspools in our toilets. Dozens wade onto the lawn before the blocks scooping up the cleanest patches in their washtubs. A sign at the block entrance reads, "Please do not eat the snow! -Mgmt" Realize I can't handle another glimpse of that poster in the chow hall today, so I skip dinner. Once Orlin's gone I hang the curtain and strip completely naked. Block's cleared out there's a precious, momentary silence. I grab up a big white handful from my tub. Hard, almost sharp. I'm exhausted. This has been the most exhausting day. Aloud, meekly, in the mirror: "Seven thousands, five hundred, forty-three more days. Please. Please, let it be better tomorrow. Just let it be better, and I can make it." I rub the snow all over me. Short gasps — it's cold, obviously. Rough. Turns my skin red and numb. But I scrub every inch. Clean my face, around my eyelids, work it into my matted hair. Along my arms, my chest, my groin, my feet. It hurts. God, it hurts. But for a second, I feel like myself. My old self. Before any of this.

When Orlin's back, he's practically gushing: "No more leak!" Parading about the cell: "It's a Bentham miracle! Leak be gone—we're saved!" Well, that's something.

Thursday, March 12th

Today's mood is: bleh. Nondescript. Disengaged, maybe. Is this our new reality, Future Self? I'm so done with it all. Seems the entire place has been blanketed in acceptance overnight. Everyone's basically calmed down. Guess they just want to carry on with their work-outs and card games and hustles. Have the porta-potties running like clockwork. Regular cooler deliveries, mugs only and names checked off after each fill-up. Has my life always been dominated by mundane needs? Survival? Back when I wanted to study and write and improve myself—were those all phantom urges? One long, cruel dream? Because none of it seems to matter much anymore. Even these entries have a whiff of futility about them... just realizing as I sit here that for March my calendar shows Blake's depiction of the ninth plague, Darkness O'er Ægypt beneath a harrowing, inky sky, Pharoah lies curled among palace shadows, his face contorted in anguish. A caption below:

"Then the LORD said to Moses, Stretch out your hand toward the sky so that darkness will spread over Egypt darkness that can be felt."

Orlin's pretty chipper, anyway. Managed to trade off one of his ridiculous, sexually-explicit dragon sketches for a pack of rolling papers. "Thank God it didn't come to smoking those Gospels!" Trying to be more patient with him, after yesterday's gesture. Plus, he talked our other neighbors Speegle and Pflugmacher into letting us run some extension cords next door, so we can watch a little TV again. Just in time, too: we're on the local news this morning—their first mention of the water crisis. They say three million gallons have been lost, all from a faulty two-inch valve. I perk up, awaiting the chilling exposé into prison conditions, but all they show is a brief interview with the town's mayor crosscut with the same old Bentham B-roll. He's requested increased local and state police patrols in the area, just as a precaution. And how are things inside? He has no earthly idea, but compliments the "fine staff", and is sure that "all needs are being met." Translation: don't you worry about it, hasn't gotten so bad they're scaling the fences." It hits me that there will never be any real accounting of this week. Probably just some puff piece drawn up in the P.R. dept. down at Central Office. Posted on the website, sent around to all the papers. Bet they'll even give the Superintendent some hokey award, honoring her "leadership and calm demeanor." That's history for you, penned by power.

Ever since breakfast, when we all spotted the tiny work crews dangling off the tower, the rumor mill has been in overdrive. Some are saying water will be restored today, others that it'll still take weeks. Or that it won't be safe to drink regardless — contaminated with chemicals or sewage or crime-reducing mind-control nanobots. No matter the outcome, I'm guessing suspicions will linger for years. A covenant had been vitiated. Faith in the First World infrastructure irreparably shaken. But of course we'll drink it, whether it's mountain-spring clear or rusty as sludge — days from now when the coolers are gone. What choice will we have?

With the leak contained and repairs in motion, there's actually to be limited movement today — some programs and religious services, morning yard. Even, according to a bulletin on the block channel, a memorial service "to honor the passing of Farley Macilwraith." Heard the Administration hated these things. They were too-blatant reminders of flawed oversight. Too potentially... humanizing. Emotional. Even subversive — as if one could shirk his punishment merely by dying. Apparently, they'd fought for a single, year-end service to cover all deceased inmates, but the Deacon insisted on individual memorials, a final act of dignity for the dead, and a chance for those left behind to grieve semi-properly. Usually, 2-3 people got squeezed into one anyway, but it must have been a slow couple months — today was just for Farley.

That afternoon, there's probably twenty-some people in the chapel. Less than I expected, considering what a man-about he was. And only recognize maybe half of these — Cray and some others from the block. Drum Circle's leading the service, I guess. Chairs are lined up on either side of the big drum. Someone hands me a program as I'm heading in. Has a photo of Farley on the front, his most recent biannual mugshot. Makes sense they'd use that one — there are no photos of life or activity here, no social media posts. Only memories, and those always fade before long. Can you even remember what he looked like, F.S.? Try. I'll wait. I bet it's just some sad, foggy muddle.

All the Native guys assemble around the drum, eight of them. The first pound is shocking, the communal chant. Never anticipated the chapel having such good acoustics. Sound of it all's so unexpected, so unusual, that I almost laugh. And the silence after is overwhelming, sort of... terrifying, actually. When the old man stands, he clears his throat and tells a story about the trickster god Coyote, who, amid some scheme to purloin a basket of pine nuts or something, inadvertently crafts death as it's still known today. In a bitter twist, Coyote's son is the first to die, and Coyote's obliged to go home and explain the situation to the poor boy's mother. "Dead?" his wife complains. "What nonsense is 'death' now?" "How might I describe him to you?" the old man as Coyote continues. "He no longer needs the air in his lungs, or meat in his stomach. You can no longer see him, or speak with him. He no longer walks about." Coyote's wife begins sobbing from this news, it's so horrible. "Let me... perhaps describe it better. Our son travels westward on a long journey. He seeks the Great Mystery, Wakan Tanka." "But he took none of his things!" she wails. "On this journey, he needs no things." "Not even his bow? His prized deerskin tunic or beaded belts?" "Only his spirit travels, while his body sleeps in the earth. But do not despair, someday we will follow him home to the Source of All Things." Do our mistakes follow us to such a place, I wonder? Does our pain?

Next comes the Sharing of Memories ("Please limit to 4 mins each"). I sink in my chair—the bulletin said nothing about public speaking. There's another long silence. No one wants to be the first to open up. To show vulnerability. Finally, some dope stands, actually chuckles, "Guess the drum should've tipped me off, but I thought they were running Protestant Services over here today... But, you know, I knew this guy! We went through Classification together years ago. Too bad." Another dope: "I didn't know... (looking at program)... Farley? Am I saying that right? But I was moved by his passing. No one should have to go through that, feel so alone and hopeless. So I'm vowing from this day forward—and we all should, really—to look out for other people. Us cons gotta stick together." Gag, F.S., Farley would've hated this. His life, or death, whatever, inspiring this proactiveness, this brotherly love from strangers? Now Cray's up telling some story about a prison-wide chess tournament, he's practically blubbering. Starting to feel so uneasy here, so... dismal. All these dinky little impressions — are these what are left of a person? What would anyone remember about a loner like me? Who would even show? And besides, I can't even recognize this person they're describing. A happy-go-lucky, all-inclusive, skip-in-his-step Farley? Who was that? He was as complicated as anybody else. Bitter, cynical. Capable of bad things and good. I'm one of the few who hasn't spoken yet. Can feel the pressure mounting. I try polishing a statement in my head — needs to be just right, do him justice, not like the word vomit all these other guys are spouting. Finally feel I've got it. Settle on: "I am a loner. Always have been. At a stage in my life of terrible solitude, Farley took the time, made the effort, to befriend me. I'll always appreciate that. He was a complex person, and his endearing qualities were not always his best ones. We ate over 3,000 meals together. Thank you." Okay. I could say that. But just as I'm standing, the drum starts again. A laboring heartbeat. The Circle moaning, keening. I slump back down. The song is the saddest I've ever heard. Only the old man seems to be singing actual words. The program has two columns of lyrics, one in English and the other in whatever language he's speaking, and I try to follow along with my finger. "Mercy, Father!" he howls. "My spirit starves! There's nothing in this whole world to satisfy me!" I foresee my prison future: long, bleak, directionless. Crushed beneath the weight of my actions. Too much, F.S. Get me out of here — I'm slipping out the back as all the wretched moans taper off. The beat lifts, becomes almost blissful: I think they're showing him off. Or me.

Speed walking back to the block, the rolled-up program's still clutched in my sweaty hand. The sun's so bright today, reflecting off the pockmarked lawns of snow. I'm gonna lose it. Why did I put myself through that? Think about this time I saw Farley running laps at yard. His bum knee slid out of place and he collapsed on the track, cursing and beating the ground. Rushed over to wait with him for the Medical cart, and it just sort of slipped out, "Jesus, doesn't that hurt?" But he ignored me, sat there gritting his teeth, the thinnest film of tears almost glazing his eyes, steeling himself with, "Don't you do it. Don't you do it." There's hardly anyone waiting for the toilets anymore. No one scavenging for snow. Everyone must have gone to yard. Thankfully, Orlin did too. Cell's empty. Looks like he even set out his razor and shaving gel in a bout of wishful thinking. I hang the curtain. Lean on the sink. I just need a little alone time. That's all. Wash my face, re-center. The me in the mirror taunts: "Just us, again." I hold in the sink buttons, so heavy. I'm drained. There's a slow-building, faraway gurgle. A rumbling. My lip trembles.

Second Prize, Fiction

The Last Time I Saw Chet

SAM JENKINS

Last night I called my dog over and over, needing to put her in for the night, and I thought again of the last time I saw Chet. The last time I saw Chet, I was married to someone I am not married to now, and I lived in a different city, although it was not the city where Chet lived. You see, Chet was, or is perhaps, my ex-wife's step-grandfather. Do you need a minute to figure that out? In today's world, it is not terribly complicated. No diagrams necessary. Every so often, we, my then-wife and then-son (I never cared for the step notation), and I would travel a few hours east to visit her grandmother and Chet. My ex-wife would get to see her grandmother, whom they called Mee-Maw. Mee-Maw would get to see her great-grandchild (who she treated as the great, grand child), and I would get to see Chet. I took an instant liking to him. Chet was that typical example of the passing generation that was not typical anymore. He had fought in two wars, managed a nuclear power plant and two different political offices. He raised three children;

two of them had reached great heights of responsible manhood and were in general, pillars of the community. The third was so beautiful that some unstable man decided he should kill her rather than lose her to another. You will have to forgive me for being short on details. Facts came scant and scattered, offered up here and there by Chet and others. I seldom pry.

On our trips to Chet's, he would take me around the grounds and show me his barn, animals, and woodworking tools. We would sit on the porch and talk; I would ask him questions and he would give me detailed answers. Then the procession would pass, led by my then-son and wife with Mee-Maw acting as the caboose. Mee-Maw would pat me on the shoulder and say, "Honey, he can't hear a word you're saying." When they were gone, Chet would resume the conversation as though nothing had happened.

I was involved in a few family gatherings at Chet's house, not as many as you might think, but still quite a few. My ex-wife's extended family, for the most part, seemed to patronize or ignore Chet, which incidentally is how you could describe their treatment of me. After all, Chet and I were additions to the family, addendums if you will. He, the octogenarian, second husband of the matriarch, who had taken the spot of the deceased, lionized, idolized, and deified grandfather, whom I had never met. I was the rough-around-the-edges husband of the thirty-year-old problem child that they had all despaired of helping and handling and had abdicated the idea that a man ever would.

Chet and I had watched football together before; he knew a lot about the game. When we would watch with her family, I would make a comment on the game, and they would look at me strangely. Later someone would make the very same comment and they would all acknowledge what a great observation it was. Chet would say nothing at all. He had learned the ropes that were wearing me out.

One time my son (I still feel that way) was in the pasture, while Chet and I were looking over his latest barn addition. I heard a commotion and my son crying. I turned around and saw a kind of pygmy horse that had knocked him down and was raring up to stomp him while a second horse was coming to its aid. I rushed at the tiny horses, scaring them to no avail. They immediately turned and fled. I turned around to see Chet dusting off the crying child and taking him in his arms. Later, I asked my son to recount what happened, expecting to be regaled with a three-year-old's take on my heroic efforts. He said, "I was trying to feed my horsey, and he knocked me down." "Then what?" I prompted. "Then," he said in an awed tone, "Chet saved me."

But, I was going to talk about the last time I saw Chet: it was at the Christmas celebration at his house, which was not on Christmas. It was on New Year's Day, I think, or maybe the day before or after, whenever that brood of vipers could congregate. The tree was up, and we watched the children open their gifts. Then came the giving and receiving of gifts to and from adults I either did not know well enough to like or knew just enough to dislike. The children were enlisted as Santa's elves to deliver the presents. My ex-wife hovered over her son's every move. I was seated next to my confederate, Chet. They brought me something, a sweatshirt I think, and I thanked whoever was responsible. Then they, accompanied by my then-mother-in-law, brought Chet a box. "This is from us," Alice said, patting him on the shoulder as he nodded his thanks. Chet took his time opening it and finally produced a pair of flannel pajamas. He turned to me, half lifting them out of the box, and said, "These are nice; who got me these?" "Roger and Alice," I said, giving a point. "Thanks," he said in their direction.

The celebration continued, and as I watched the children disbursing gifts, Chet tapped me on the shoulder. "Who got me these pajamas?" he asked. I paused, "Alice and Roger gave you those." "Hmmph," he responded looking into the box. I talked briefly with one of my then-wife's cousins about a local football team. When I was done, Chet tapped me again. "Who gave me these?" he asked, his hands shakily going through the clothing. I swallowed hard

"Roger and Alice," I said in a whisper.

I had not seen Chet for at least three months before that. I had missed Thanksgiving; I think she and I were fighting of course. We were always fighting. I had no idea. In the next hour, he received many gifts and I repeatedly fielded his numerous inquisitions as to their origins.

Later that night, Mee-Maw told Chet he needed to get the dog out of the pasture and put her in the garage for the night. "It is cold and Maggie gives the horses a hard time if we leave her out there," she explained to the crowd. Then she asked me if I minded going with him.

We walked to the pasture, and Chet unlocked the gate and latched it back behind us. Maggie was romping through the pasture and proved to be a reluctant captive. We had to go to the garage and get food with which to lure her. Maggie apprehended, I walked her outside the gate, my hand clasped closely around her collar. Chet stood beside me and patted the pockets of his coat and pants. "Have you got the lock?" he asked me. I replied, "No." "I must have dropped it somewhere back there," he said looking at the pasture. I dragged Maggie, halting, balking, and barking to the garage. We put her on a tether, placed food in her bowl, grabbed two flashlights, and headed back to the enclosure. I walked one side of the area we had been in while Chet walked the other. We met up in the middle and I asked him if he had seen anything. "No, there is no telling where it is," he said, placing his left hand on his hip and pushing his coat back slightly. "Chet, what's that bulge in your breast pocket?" I asked. "Huh?" he said, producing the lock.

Once we were back on the outside of the gate, Chet began to affix the lock, and then paused. "Did you turn on the electricity?" he asked. I headed to the barn to turn on the electric fence switch that ran in front of the chain link fence along with the barbed wire that discouraged the diminutive horses from tearing it apart as a pastime. I threw the switch and returned to the gate watching the exhale of my breath in the early January night.

Once again on the outside of the gate, he stood there watching me expectantly. "You have the lock, don't you Chet?" I asked, my tone becoming abrasive. "I thought you had it," he said. "Check your pockets," I told him while he looked at me beseechingly, hands thrust deeply in his coat pockets. "I already did," he said. Admittedly, I was agitated at this point and I frisked him as roughly as any Irish beat cop had ever aspired to. The lock was not in his pockets. Disheartened, I turned on the flashlight and saw the lock laying by his feet. "I'll get it," Chet offered. "No," I responded, perhaps too quickly, "I will lock it up." "Hold on a minute," Chet said, "I need to turn the electric fence on."

When we returned, Mee-Maw asked, "What took you boys so long?" "Maggie didn't much care for being put up," I responded. She rolled her eyes for the benefit of her clan. "It took the two of you that long to put up sweet little Maggie?" Now, Maggie was neither sweet nor little, but I chose not to respond. As we drove back through the darkness and the child slept, I told my wife what had happened. I did not cry back then, but on the inside, I felt like I could. I wanted to cry for Chet. We propelled forward through the night. She took my hand, her eyes filling up with tears, as she told me about the things she had noticed about Chet. We discussed how neither of us had felt compelled to say anything to the others. I steered with my left hand as she rested her head on my shoulder. A rare moment of both peace and intimacy for us. We took turns looking at our slumbering son resting in his trust, assuming our steadiness, and that we would deliver him where he needed to be. He had no other choice.

I stood there in the darkness calling out her name, wondering where she was at.

The wife and I, the then-wife and I, eventually split up, of course. Looking back, I don't know what convinced either one of us that we could live in matrimonial harmony. Neither of us had ever lived in harmony with anything, especially each other.

We were so much alike. I think that was both what drew us together and what pulled us apart. Opposite poles that pull on each other until they swap places, and now the powers that repel them are stronger than ever.

I remember sitting in that coffee shop listening to her tell me a little about herself, and it had might as well been my story. We had dropped out of college an equal number of times, struggled with many of the same things. We had thrown away the same opportunities, destroyed those that were precious, lived in hope of a newness, and some sort of miracle of control. I soon barreled through life with new confidence, as if I had found the piece that completed the puzzle, for a while.

Once, when we were discussing how much alike we were, she said, "But opposites attract, right?" I said, "We are opposites, I am the positive and you are the negative." She hated that, who wouldn't?

You always think you will know when it happens, but you don't. When you fall apart, when all your abilities to manage, navigate, and remedy are rendered worthless. You think, at the least, in retrospect you would be able to pinpoint the place in time where everything was okay but after that it was a downhill slide to oblivion. The truth is it happens so gradually you cannot recognize, nevermind contain, it. Perhaps it was all there from the beginning, all the forces that were going to destroy me, us. The emotions, the bitterness and unforgivingness, romping around loose and hungry, ready to devour. Our shallow pride ready to stomp the other one at the least sign of weakness to raise our status in our own eyes.

The house had become a war zone. We fought the same battles, I mean the very same battles. We would have a new argument, and then the old ones would come up. The child walked through this every day rolling his eyes, seemingly unaffected. This was his normal. I felt like I was shakily going over the same evidence, combing over the same facts, yet again unable to draw a conclusion. We ran over the same ground, lashing out at one another with the same words until I wanted to scream, "Roger and Alice bought you the pajamas. Nothing has changed. It will always be the same?"

I stood in the nearly empty house wondering where it went wrong. Was it all wrong from the beginning? The house built on the slope sliding toward its inevitability. Or, was it my fault? Could I have averted it? Did I forget something? Had I changed some bad behavior or discharged some withheld action, would it have been different? Had I held the key all along and just misplaced it? Walking out of the pasture with the lock in my pocket, defeated. The gate open behind me, leaving cruel dogs loose and unfed and tiny destructive horses running wild.

I called her name again and again. I stood there staring westward, wondering where she was at or what might have become of her.

I left the garage door open, poured some food into the bowl. Finally, I closed the door and went to bed.

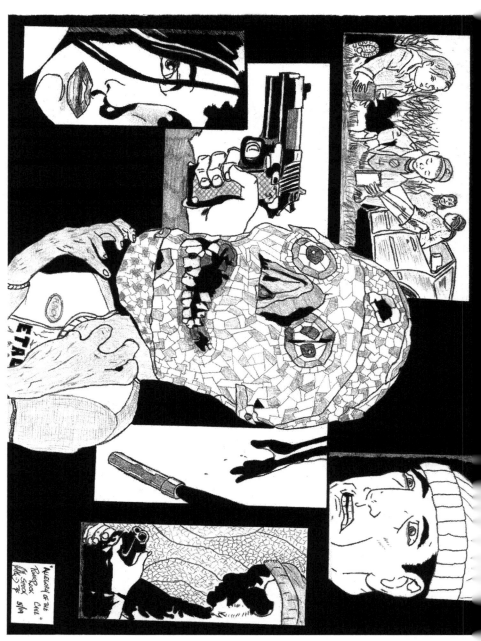

Illustration by Jeremy Wils

Third Prize, Fiction

Geode
DAVID A. PICKETT

Randy picked up a geode — a black, gnarled rock, sliced open to reveal a crystalline pocket within — and turned it over in his hands. It was weird, such an ugly exterior concealing a wonder within. He nearly dropped it when the woman spoke behind him.

"Couldn't get enough, huh?"

His mouth dry from nerves, Randy swallowed, set the rock back on the gift shop shelf, and turned around to face the tour guide. He was lanky, awkward in a body he'd seemingly never grown into. He looked like a thirty-year-old teenager, in his worn jeans and unzipped sweatshirt over a faded Metallica T-shirt, from the days when he and Diane still went to concerts, before marriage and kids. He tightened his ponytail nervously, then shoved his hands in the pockets of his sweatshirt — one of which crackled from an empty shopping bag — and smiled briefly.

"Yeah, I wanted to take a few more pictures. I liked that room with all the, uh — " He couldn't remember the names, there had been so many names; he mimed columns with his hands.

"Stalactites? Stalagmites?"

"Those! They were cool."

The guide smiled and looked around. "Where are the kids? Are they coming too?"

"My wife has a headache, so she's not going, and Coop and Teeny wanted a picnic, so..." He trailed off. Mentally, Randy cursed at himself; he didn't want to share any identifying information, like names. Even if they were nicknames, they were too close to the originals, Cooper and Tina. Their "picnic" consisted of bologna and Wonder Bread sandwiches washed down with warm Pepsi, out in the parking lot. He hoped that Diane was coping with them okay. She had a tendency to get snappish, especially when she overheated, and their van had no air conditioning.

"Well, we're glad to have you back. We'll head down in just a couple of minutes."

The entrance to the caves was at the back of the gift shop. Randy trailed the rest of the tour group, a dozen or so people, down the stone steps that led into the caverns below. He stepped gingerly, back painful and threatening to spasm, despite the oxycodone he had taken just a couple of hours before. A fall from a roof had left him unable to work, at least as a roofer, and he refused to apply down at the Wal-Mart despite Diane's urging. They were making it, if just barely, on her home health aide pay and his disability, and if it hadn't been for her sister's wedding—the reason for their road trip—he wouldn't have been so desperate for money. Diane's family had always looked down on him. He had come from the poor side of town, and even when he'd been working, he hadn't been able to support the family to his in-laws' standards. Randy couldn't face showing up to his sister-in-law's wedding without a gift, and, even worse, maybe having to ask for help with gas money to get back home. He couldn't face the expression on his mother-in-law's face, the unsurprised disappointment of Diane's father.

The guide's bright flashlight beam played over the walls as they descended, adding to the weak yellow light cast by battery-powered lamps mounted on metal boxes along the way.

The tour group went down the steps and through the tunnels, while the guide pointed out features of the caves, reeling off her polished spiel about geologic time and the corrosive effects of water on limestone. Randy had heard it all already, of course. He hung back, at the tail end of the group, hands in his pockets. He avoided making eye contact with any of the others.

They went through the Spillway, the Map Room, the Cathedral with its columns of stone and colored mineral deposits mimicking stained glass, where he took several pictures with his phone, not bothering to look at the results. After the Dragon's Lair, with its glittering throat leading to further, inaccessible wonders, they reached the Galaxy Room. As they entered this cavern, where the ceiling opened out and the walls pulled back to make a large open space, Randy moved past the rest of the group to stand near the guide, who had her hand on the lamp box mounted on the wall. The rest of the tour group milled around, and she raised her voice to be heard over the murmur. Echoes reflected her every word.

"This is the Galaxy Room. You may be wondering why we call it that, when it's a cave deep underground, while the galaxy—our galaxy, the Milky Way—is far above, in the night sky, invisible from here. I'm about to turn out the lights and show you.

"Now, be careful—don't try and walk around when I turn the lights off. We don't want anyone to fall and get hurt. Also, your phones and cameras may not be able to capture what you're about to see. Please don't use flashes. They won't help and they'll ruin the experience for others."

Randy was sweating heavily. He shifted a step closer to the guide, who smiled at him. She flipped a switch to turn the lamp off, then clicked off the flashlight. The ceiling of the cavern sprang to phosphorescent life. What had been dull gray was now marked with sprays and swirls of glowing colors, pinks and greens and purples, as if the ceiling had been painted with light. It didn't much look like the Milky Way; it was a more fantastic collection, like glowing nebulas, clouds of stardust and remnants of supernovas, splashed across otherwise starless space.

Randy pulled the pistol out of his sweatshirt pocket and pointed it at the tour guide. He spoke in a low voice. "Give me the flashlight."

At first she didn't seem to understand what was happening. She said, "It'll just be a couple of minutes, then I'll turn the lights back on."

"Give me that flashlight," he said, voice slightly raised, and he waved the pistol in her direction. He realized she couldn't see it. "I have a gun," he said, his voice cracking slightly on the last word. His stomach was churning and he felt like throwing up. He just wanted this whole thing to be over, to be back out on the road with the windows down and the wind blowing through, with Randy Travis on the radio singing about a barbecue.

"What?" the guide said, her voice rising. There was a click, and the flashlight came on.

The sudden light startled Randy, and he nearly dropped the gun. He waved it at her again.

"Give me that light!"

Most of the group was oblivious to what was happening. They were still looking around the cavern, talking to one another about what they'd just seen. One woman, however, had noticed. She saw the pistol in Randy's hand and uttered a little scream. She clutched at the arm of the man she was with.

Randy's gut spasmed. He raised his voice and spoke to the entire group. "Hey, people. This is a robbery." He cleared his throat. "I need your wallets and your money. And gimme that damn flashlight!" He poked the pistol toward the guide, who had gone very pale. She handed over the flashlight.

Randy took the light and lodged it under an armpit, then reached into his pocket and pulled out a plastic grocery bag. He handed it to the guide and said, "Get everybody's stuff in that."

One old man had sat on the floor of the cave, massaging his chest. Others pulled out their wallets and handed them to the guide. A woman tried to give the guide a large purse, and Randy realized that there was no way it was going to fit in the bag. He called out, "Just wallets and cash, people. I don't need no damn purses."

It seemed to take forever. Randy was wet with sweat by the time the guide brought the bag back to him. It was lumpy and it jingled — people had put coins in, too — and he almost dropped the flashlight when he grabbed the handles from the guide.

"All right, people, you all just stay put, I'm going to go on up and get out of here. I want you to wait fifteen minutes before you move from this room. Got that?" He waved the pistol at the group. There was a general murmur of assent. He wasn't worried about them phoning for help; there was no signal down here, in the depths.

"Can I turn the lamp back on?" the guide asked.

"Once I leave you can." Randy backed up toward the exit to the cavern. The old man had lain back on the rock, his blue-haired companion cradling his head in her lap. She was bent over and seemed to be talking to him in low voice. Randy backed out of the room, turned, and fled toward the exit. Behind him, the lamp flickered on.

Randy shoved the gun back into his pocket, and moved rapidly through the last caves, stopping at each lamp box to turn it off. It wouldn't slow them down much, he figured, but it was something. It was in the next to last room, when he switched off the lamp and turned to leave, that he tripped over a stone ridge in the floor, sending the flashlight skittering across the floor and dropping the plastic bag. The flashlight went out. Coins rolled across the floor, and Randy's back erupted in pain, as if molten steel had been poured down his spinal cord. He let out a small scream.

He stayed down on his hands and knees, in the dark, for several minutes, hoping the pain would subside, would relent enough to allow him to get up. It did not. He laid down on the floor, on his side, knees drawn up toward his chest. Hot tears rolled across the bridge of his nose and dripped onto the rocky floor of the cave. He thought about Diane, sitting up in their minivan, sweating in the heat; about Teeny and Coop, eating limp bologna sandwiches and waiting for their dad to show up; about his mother- and father-in-law, when they heard the news. He reached into his sweatshirt pocket and pulled the pistol out. He waited for a light.

Fielding Dawson Prize, Fiction

Fireside: or Immaterial Burns

DAVID WEBB

It was a warm and breezy, sunny day near the end of summer. The wind was strong but there was no chill with it. It was what some considered perfect weather. Tyrone, a man in his mid 30s, he was thinking: so far so good. As he had had only one drink, and it was well after noon. He didn't even feel like he needed another one- not even a little bit.

Tyrone was standing near the corner of Lafayette and Division, in front of the painted yellow brick tenement- blanketed with autographs-, across from the old sooty bricked, windowless Roanoke warehouse, watching the big-headed boy, Joe D, his lil' main man, steadily approach, and he liked how it felt feeling the distance continuing to close between them. He wore a cloudy gray silk shirt that billowed each time the wind had blown, Jordace jeans, and lizard skinned lace-ups.

Tyrone stayed sharp; he always made sure of it. Even last month, when he was drinking like a fish- boozing like an undisputed alcoholic.

And, the funny thing about that is, he thought then that he was about to get better. He recognized afterward, that it had been—not exactly hopeless, but—a complete failure, exactly the opposite of what he had intended. It wouldn't stop him from trying again and again and again, though. It couldn't.

Nevertheless, he wasn't thinking about any of that stuff right now. It was thinking about it that made it bad, made him do himself wrong.

He was watching the boy step up on the curb—smiling, like he couldn't comprehend the boy's pitiful expression. The boy's right hand was bandaged with gauze and tape. He was only eight years old, but healthy enough to appear several years older, in cut off shorts, suede Puma basket tennis shoes, and a white t-shirt. He was walking with his head down, about to pass by, when Tyrone stopped him.

"Joe D," he said. "What's going on, lil' man? Hinh? You wasn't going to stop and holler at me?"

The boy turned and looked over his shoulder, up Lafayette, to see if he would find his mother leaning out of the window, looking after him.

"I gotta go the store for my mother," the boy, Joe D said.

"R-ight man," said Tyrone, still smiling, and noticing the boy's bandaged hand. "You still playing ball? Hinh?"

He squeezed the boy's shoulder. Not sure if he was aware that something was wrong, and having yet to receive a response, Tyrone continued to question him.

"You work on the low post move I showed you? Hinh? Hinh?"

"Yeah. Yeah..." the boy said, unable to remain unaffected by the man's excitement about him and the game.

"They can't stop me," he concluded.

He had been about to walk off again, when Tyrone held him in place with the hand on his shoulder.

"Hold on," Tyrone told him.

A small gray Mazda pulled up, along the outside of the car between it and Tyrone and the boy, Joe D. It was Tyrone's friend. A nice looking woman, despite harsh looking eyes and heavy brows, with freshly permed big-hair and a lot of jewelry.

"He didn't know," he responded to what she had asked him. Then he turned his back on her; and she frowned, mumbled something distastefully, and pouted for a while before pulling off. And the boy, Joe D, he watched her car until it turned off at Pennsylvania Avenue, wondering if he'd have girls driving around looking for him when he was bigger.

"Hey…" Tyrone was saying to the boy, who was looking back over his shoulder again. "Where you been? I aint seen you in a good lil' while."

The boy looked up at Tyrone; he knew what a 'good lil' while' meant. He had only been punished the day before; and the day before that, Tyrone had given him a pocket full of change to play video games. He'd known what it was to see someone drunk, too. Now he had a better idea of what it was to be drunk. Still, he wasn't going to let Tyrone's being sober stop him from believing he wouldn't be as generous now.

He lowered his big head, and in a childish voice intended to provoke pity, Joe D told Tyrone, "I been punished."

"Again," Tyrone replied, disbelievingly. "Who your mother think she is… the warden?"

And afterward, he dug into Joe D's ribs, trying to make him laugh. But it didn't work.

"Look," he said, holding up his bandaged hand for inspection.

"What happened?" Tyrone asked, genuinely concerned.

" I got caught playing with matches again," the boy told him.

"Matches, "Tyrone repeated. "Again. Boy…"

A sharp, bitter taste filled Tyrone's sinuses, cutting off his speech, causing his nose to run, and his eyes to glaze over. He swallowed hard, feeling the thing inside that caused his pain to grow.

"Oh shit," Tyrone said. "Again."

He removed some coins from his pocket and gave them to the boy; before patting him on the head, and telling him, "Go the store for your mother."

Tyrone stood still for some time—seeing nothing; feeling faint and helpless; angry and cursed; like some undesirable force was keeping him from going crazy, and freeing him from the madness. And he couldn't take it anymore.

So he made his way around the corner, on Division, where he leaned against the passenger's side door of his car and, with his elbows on the hood, he stared at the shinny pieces embedded in the street reflecting the sunlight; while he continued to try and gather some strength, before getting in.

Inside his car, a money green Seville, not yet a year old, the smell of the cream colored leather interior replaced the pissy stench of the phone booth he passed when he turned off Lafayette. Of the four or five trees all on the one side of Division, Tyrone had always parked his car under the biggest, whose branches hung well enough over the car so that those people—in front of whose house his car was parked—couldn't come to their front window and look down and see what he was doing.

Tyrone reached under the seat and pulled out a half pint. He broke the seal and he hit it hard. He tightened the cap back, unpursed, and quickly licked his wet lips. The liquor warmed his body, and it felt good; so good, that he moved his toes in his shoes; and, for a minute, he forgot about the boy, and what he himself had done. It was all pushed back a little.

Just a little. Then it was back again.

The leather strained as Tyrone leaned forward to push in the cigarette lighter, and again, when he sat back in the seat. He shook a cigarette up from the pack, removed it with his mouth, and dropped the pack on the seat beside him. Then he waited patiently for the lighter to pop out.

Tyrone lit his cigarette. He drew hard, inhaled, and exhaled; and before the fumes had finished leaving his nose, he was drawing on the cigarette again; while looking for the boy, Joe D, to show up in his rearview.

Tyrone continued smoking. The smoke scattered, like powder, as it filtered out of the open window and into the wind. He rubbed his temple while contemplating the boy's hand, and he took another sip.

Did she? Tyrone wondered. Did the goody two shoes up in the window do that?

Tyrone took a long last draw on his cigarette and plucked the butt out of the window. He tried to picture the wise and righteous look on her face as she held her boy's hand over a flame; and, he took another sip. The boy was bad, Tyrone thought, looking at what was left in the bottle. Just a few weeks before, he had found the boy in the alley with a thirteen year old girl; the lie ready on his lips: "We wasn't doing nothing." He smiled as he recalled it. But now the boy was playing with fire. And with that old, blind man in the house, who, from age alone, would have plenty of trouble getting around. And, thinking he understood something of the woman's intuition, he considered: if you weighed the blind old man and the lives of the boy's entire family against his fingers; then, you could see...

But how did she know? And where did she gain the wisdom? Tyrone wondered.

Tyrone began thinking about the past twenty-five years of his life. He thought about how his father would materialize out of nowhere; and how he would see him before all of his friends, and run away from where they were playing, with his friends calling after him, wondering what was wrong. Why was he running from his father? And no matter how far or fast he ran, wherever he stopped, his father would always be right there; sometimes feigning panting, but always smelling like liquor. Always with the same speech about how much he loved him, his brother, and his mother; and about him being the only one that would talk to him, the only one that believed him, when he said that he didn't burn that house down.

Tyrone finished the bottle.

Not long afterward, he saw the big-headed boy, Joe D, in his rearview, walking with head down and his mother's bag in his hand.

He thought about his own mother — about how much he wanted to tell her, last month, after visiting his father's grave. But he couldn't — knew he never would. Because he'd thought about telling her before; a lot earlier, when he had first taken on some responsibility. When his father's pitiful, drunken face, and restrainedly imploring tone effected him the most.

Now, and not for the first time, he reflected on the possibility that, maybe his mother had been happier without his father. A drunk, who came home every evening after work, and drank until he fell asleep on the living room floor; before going to work the next day, and doing the same thing all over again and again and again. There was no big change in her behavior, he reasoned.

Maybe she knew already, and was as wise as lil' Joe D's mother had been.

Tyrone got out his keys. He started his car. The plan to talk to the boy's mother was off, because, he said to himself, I'm drunk. But he would, he thought — pulling out of the space and turning the Cadillac back towards Lafayette — buy himself another half pint, and go somewhere where the woman in the Mazda couldn't find him; and there, he would sit and sip and wonder, how the boy's mother knew that it would be best for him to be the only victim. When he could figure something out — something that didn't conflict with what his mother was teaching him, he would tell the boy, Joe D, his lil' main man, what he knew about fire, and about immaterial burns.

I don't pretend to know why everyone writes in prison, but I do know that writing helps process trauma, and trauma is the common denominator of everyone incarcerated.

Thank you for showing up. The first step to changing what is not working or fair or right—is to hear another side of a story. Thank you for listening and being open to hearing about another's experience.

Sometimes one conversation, one phone call, one raised hand can crack open a door, can cause something to be revisited, can give someone a chance.

Include pieces from prisoners in your forums.
Include us in your publications.
Include us in your conversations.
Include us.

— Elizabeth Hawes
2015-2019 Multi-Prize winner in Poetry, Drama, and Memoir,
PEN America Prison Writing Awards

2019 PEN AMERICA PRISON WRITING AWARDS IN **POETRY**

First Prize, Poetry

All of Us, In Prison

JEVON JACKSON

Some prisons are pistol-thick,
core-earth dense
with a long electric fence that wraps
around,
and some prisons are softer
than the molecules in muslin,
as it drapes across the bundled bed,
clinging to your body;

Some prisons taste like
salt, copper, sludge
when you bite and crunch down
to the marrow,
and some prisons are
Gorgonzola
and challah bread,
enough to comfort you
from leaving;

Some prisons sit on ominous hills,
hundreds of miles from where
your mother, brother, daughter lives,
and some prisons are closer than
the whip speed of electrochemicals
that dodge collisions in the brain;

Some prisons have
unassuming names, like this:
Havenworth, Hiker's Island, Eagle's Bay,
The New Lisbon Correctional Institute,
and some prisons
are simply called by their
God-fearing names:
Heroin, Oxycontin, Vodka, Blackjack,
Molested For Years By Him;

some prisons, by the night,
will never let you go,and some prisons, in the light, will never let you go.

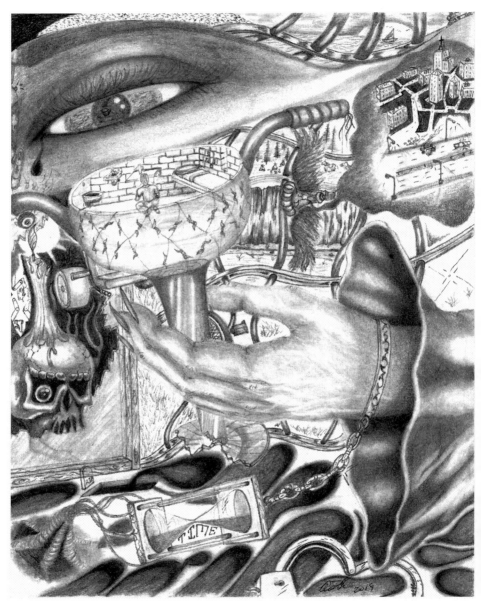

Illustration by Andrew Romero

Time Reversal Invariance

DAVID A. PICKETT

Time reversal invariance fails for the decay of the K meson, or kaon.
(David Deutsch, The Road to Reality)

It used to be that physicists
thought the world might run
the same forward as in reverse:
that is to say, we had no means
to know which way time flowed.
In such a world, a stream where
we were carried against the current
of our lives, cartwheeled up the slope
of our personal avalanches––
the whock-whock-whock of helicopter blades
scooped the air between crash site
and yellow cross on hospital roof
led directly to the black stench
of burning rubber and the glittering ice
of glass pebbles cast among the highway
shoulder's muted gray gravel and
the confusing geometry of the wreck:
limbs askew, bent at obtuse angles,
isosceles triangles excised from fleshy parts,
barred circle imprinted on the driver's chest,
hyperbolic spray of blood on the grass;
which upcoming or just past convinced
the driver to send one last text
or the first in a series which ends
as he pulls out of the driveway, headed
toward his final equation's solution
or his morning cup of coffee, dark
brewed and bitter, thick foamy liquid
straining itself back into ground beans.

Ravenous

CAROLINE ASHBY

I always run toward the sound of shouting, metal crunching
and glass shattering
My mom would wonder aloud where she went wrong in my rearing. She thought
one day she would find me in a body bag or worse, missing,
      I'd be lost. My bones, lonely,
bleached by the unyielding sun.

I hate hospitals, morgues and funeral homes although my activity
      speaks differently -
            I am the first to arrive
Mom requested only my company during her final days.
She utilized the quiet gift the feared in me while
I watched her last breath and the pulse stop in her neck.
Life was clear and sharp. Death uncovered without discrimination.

In the year after she blew with the wind and floated and sunk
      in her most private rivers,
            I attended six wakes.
We are all aware of the charade.
The cans on the shelf are straightened in hopes it will change
      the flavor of the contents

I yearned for the day my pulse would stop and I could be
      with my mom. What I didn't see happening--
      a purposeful disorganization in the Kitchen,
      product kept and unkept,
      more flavor to the unsalted
      and a stronger desire
      to live.

Honorable Mention, Poetry

Self-Portrait as State Property

P.M. DUNNE

Eleven A oh six seven one they call as the boy not quite a man
Moves further down the line like a lamb in a slaughterhouse
End of the conveyor belt a nurse tells him to drop his drawers so she
Can inspect his meat she prods and pokes he coughs and chokes but
There's nothing funny about spreading your cheeks for a stranger to gaze
Inside your asshole nothing funny about the officer's nightstick cracking
Against somebody's skull shattering their ribs because the nurse gave them
A woody the boy's beautiful dark mane is shaved before he shampoos his raw
Scalp under water like the Devil's piss and returns to the line this time
To get his picture taken his mug forever remembered in the Hall of Shame
An officer with eyes the color of tobacco spit hands him an ID:
Name Din # Eyes DOB Height Weight Hair Sex Language
But none of these things matter he is eleven A oh six seven one
Forever or at least for the next decade and a half which to him
Is the same his state greens are at least two sizes too big the others say he'll grow
Into them he looks around at the gunmetal bars the white paint the blue of the
Officers' uniforms and doesn't see how he can grow into them into it into this
How the hell do you get used to seeing men used as pincushions as cutting boards
Their mouths like gaping flounders when the officers break it up how the hell
Do you get used to breathing air thick as mildew the floors of the corridors
Speckled with the blood of decades past the sleepless nights the open
Windows in February that get closed in July the roaches inside your locker in the hole
Underneath your sink dripping with water water that reminds the boy
Of Lady Liberty of pennies of the nine volts he pressed
On his tongue as a child at his grandparent's house out of boredom
Out of a deep frustration no one including himself was aware of
He can never get used to the others the other prisoners the other men
The other kids born without last names and debating the truth
Like Jews and Christians unable to breathe because they're buried alive
Drowning in the fire in the box kicking the walls and rattling the bars
Flinging shit like chimps screaming for someone anyone to listen
Watching as the boy not quite a man Eleven A oh six seven one

My Co-worker

EDWARD JI

My co-worker makes parole.
No goodbyes. Just disappears one day.
We wish him well in our hearts,
Like among the dead, one resurrected.
He'll forget about those still dead;
Shake off the gray dust,
While here, we still sleep,
An island away from the world.
I file my departed friend
Into my memories of the gone,
And inherit his work-boots
As if I were the living,
And he the dead.

As I Hear the Rain

DOUGLAS WEED

As I hear the rain pitter-patting
On the glass like tiny tap dancers with
Their shiney steel-tipped black shoes,
I hum a little tune and wander through the green—
House tending the vegetables growing
In piles of dirt collected within
Plain unornamented brown pots,
                              She had
Never understood my fascination
With the smell of dirt and fertilizer
Trapped in rows of rotting wooden benches.
Rain streaks the neglected face glaring coldly
From the kitchen window as I move
To protect the tomatoes from the frost
That is sure to come during the night.

Illustration by Tara Layer

Honorable Mention, Poetry

Young Girl Twenty

VAUGHN WALKER

5'10 admired by crooks that be like, "Hey Dawn"
Mostly by chicks that get they hate on
Suede boots, with a Gucci skirt, she stayed
on Apple juice and Bonton chips, to keep her weight on
The type of chick that young thugs'll wait on,
and older catz lose they weight on
Modestly fly, sour chicks couldn't play Dawn
Pride and principles, she got 'em from her gay mom
Admired catz that could play calm and shoot at dudes with a straight arm...
Sorta like...AI with his game on daddy
It only took the little things to make Dawn happy
As a younger girl she remembered how drugs took chatty
Or should I say: How mommy said, "God took daddy"
She couldn't contemplate tragedy
At age 5 thinking she could climb trees if she planted apple seeds in God's eye
When no rain came she thought, "Then why try?"
When 15 came she thought, "If I die, I'ma have the phattest of whips,
of plenty catz that called me small fry"
Yeah, little Dawny had plenty features that appeal to a soft eye
At 16, Damn! They thought they'd all fry
Now Dawny all grown built like a horse riiiggghhhttt!
See, things changed when pleasure became a name
And shorty changed the game for killahs who honored fame,
Now Dawny got 'em trained...
To get money or they lame
How things change is a story's heart, but for Dawny...
5 bullets and a cop was a jealous narc

It is my hope that the literary community will see me as a woman, a writer, a voice, not as a prisoner holding a past.

— Louise K Waakaa'igan (AKA Karol House)
2017 Second Place Prize Winner in Poetry,
PEN America Prison Writing Awards

2019 PEN AMERICA
PRISON WRITING AWARDS
IN NONFICTION **MEMOIR**

First Prize, Memoir

Where the Wild Things Are

WILLIAM MYRL SMITHERMAN

The psychiatrist comports himself as a genial mantis, his long limbs snapping out to snare fresh friends for our secret and secretive community. He teaches at a university, has consulted with the FBI, and is nothing if not overqualified to be meddling in a correctional institution. His shoes are well maintained.

Our group meets in an abandoned classroom in J-building. The tables are pulled into an ugly diamond where ten offenders gather, sometimes more or less, along with the head nurse and the doctor. Established as a "medication clinic" under the aegis of the drug company that supplies the prison, it is the first and only such group in Virginia. Its existence rests solely on the workaholism of our psychiatrist, who willed it into being.

"You may have noticed we have someone new with us today... Mr. Tamil, you have a background that is unlike any I have seen, and I've been doing this a long time. In here, there are some unwritten rules:

What is said here stays in the group, there is no disrespect, and you don't have to say anything if you don't want to. Would you like to share with the group some of your story?"

Tamil was sitting at the opposing corner of the diamond. Dark-skinned and attenuated, his head was drastically torqued to one side. He could look forward but only momentarily, all the while appearing to struggle with an invisible and pitiless angel wrestling his head to the left.

"My name is Michael," he said, speaking in an accent I associate with black people being interviewed on world news. "I came from Sudan, when I was young, to this country. I have been here many years. I was arrested ten years ago for making a bad mistake. It was legal in my country."

"You are welcome to share about your offense, but you don't have to. Most people choose not to."

"Okay, okay."

"Is that a drug side effect?" Sex Offender asked. Pudgy and middle-aged, with a thin mustache and state-issued tortoise shell glasses, his voice whined. "Did that cause the problem you have with your neck?"

"It was the wrong medication," Michael said. "They gave it to me at another institution. Treatment is helping now."

Breaking and Entering had slid low in his chair next to me with his arms crossed, but this exchange brought him forward.

"The medication is called Trilafon," he said. "I was on it, too. The same thing happened to me. It locked up my side. It's got serious side effects. Luckily," he gestured to the psychiatrist, "he was able to put me on something else and fix me."

"Now, there are side effects," the psychiatrist offered, "and there are adverse effects. A side effect; we don't like to have them, but maybe someone can live with them if the medicine is doing them good. Adverse effects are different, and we will always discontinue a treatment if it has adverse effects. In the case of Trilafon, it has an acute adverse effect, where you are paralyzed. It can feel like you're dying. In that case, we do an intervention, and there is recovery. On the other hand, there is a chronic condition which requires a longer term treatment."

"Is that permanent then?" Sex Offender asked.

"It is much better than it was," Michael said. "They gave me Trilafon for six years. It was very bad."

"Trilafon can cause permanent damage in some cases," the psychiatrist said. "It has also helped a lot of people."

"So they made a mistake giving it to him," Sex Offender said.

"It wasn't the right treatment in his case. You never know for sure how someone is going to react to a drug, but there has been improvement. Mr. Tamil, would you like to tell everyone about how you came here? I think they could benefit from hearing about it."

"Okay," Michael said, then paused. "My village was gone." "Your village was attacked," the psychiatrist supplied.

"Yes," he said. "Men came and they shot everyone. All gone." His head turned forward as he spoke, then snapped back to the left. His hand was like a spider cradling his face.

"How old were you?"

"I was six and walked away, and I met others and we walked. It was very hard. We walked to Nigeria."

"It was very dangerous?"

"Yes. We were hungry, and there was no water." Hands fluttered, miming someone falling by the wayside. "There were lions. My friend, we walked together, and the lion took him."

"How did you get away?" "I ran."

"You don't have to be faster than the lion," Sex Offender said. "You just have to be faster than the next guy."

"How old was your friend," the psychiatrist asked.

"Seven or eight."

"I bet the hyenas were even worse than the lions," Sex Offender said. "They're pack hunters."

"No. The lion was worst."

"Lions are pack hunters, too," Grave Digger said. He sat beside Michael, dwarfing him. "It's the females that go out and hunt. The males lie back."

"That's right," Sex Offender said. "They defend their territory." "Got it good," Grave Digger said, nodding his huge head. "They got it real good." "We walked for three months," Michael said.

"Would you say that lions were the most dangerous kind of predator you encountered during your travel?" the psychiatrist asked Michael.

"Yes," Michael said, looking at his shoulder.

"There are other kinds of predators," the psychiatrist said. "Does anyone have an experience they could share about difficult situations they've been in?"

"Well, I was never chased by lions," Sex Offender said, "but I was in the military for twenty years. There have been bullets flying everywhere, and yeah, it's scary. I knew a lot of people that died on 9/11, a lot of good men."

Diabetes was seated next to Sex Offender. He was tall, ruddy, and dilapidated. "Guy had a knife to me one time, in Atlanta. There are streets down there you don't go down if you're white, not unless you got ten of your friends with you."

Across from him, Grave Digger dandled his enormous head over the table. "Atlanta?"

"Yeah."

"Didn't know it was like that down there. I been to Atlanta plenty of times."

"This was in the nineties. Anyway, a guy pulled out this switchblade on me in my window. He says, gimme what you got or I'm gonna kill you. I say, hold on buddy, I got my wallet for ya. It's in my pocket here, can I get it? He says, you keep your hand on the window, get your wallet with your other hand. So I reach over like this"—Diabetes mimes extending his arm with cautious sloth—"moving real slow. I've got my .357 in the seat pocket. My wallet's in the glove compartment. I reach down and get the gun and point it at him. Guy starts shaking like a leaf." He shows us with his hands. "I gave him the same choice he gave me. He can get gone or die. I give him to the count of five, and he drops the switchblade and runs."

"In Atlanta?" Grave Digger asked.

"Yeah," Diabetes said. "So I count to five and shoot into the air. Man, if he didn't drop to the ground before he was halfway across the parking lot. I never went round there again after that."

"You felt in danger of your life," the psychiatrist said.

"Yeah!" Diabetes said. "I'm six three. I'm a big guy, and this fella made me look small. Another time, me and my wife moved down to Winston-Salem cuz her dad was there. There was this arcade where the Mexicans came. They were all done up, gang members. I gave my wife a roll of quarters and told her to keep playing the game. Don't look at them. These were guys that would kill you if you looked at them the wrong way."

"In Winston-Salem?" Grave Digger said, his massive head like the bole of a twisted tree.

"Yeah."

"I never knew it."

"Yeah, they went through stuff on the counter and took whatever they wanted. They had food, bags of candy, and stuff from the shelves. The clerk held her hands up and didn't say anything. Then they left. I asked her what that was about and she said they came in sometimes. She said, 'It's not my store. As long as I don't say anything they leave me alone.' I didn't know it was like that. My father-in-law didn't say anything about that before we moved there.

"So in the house I had a dog, our guard dog. We'd brought him with us. He started barking in the middle of the night, and I go to the window and see a bunch of cars pulled up in the driveway. It was the Mexicans. I thought they were coming to get us. So I put my wife in the closet and pile up the mattresses against it, and I've got the dog in my hand trying to shut him up. These Mexicans, they've got machetes and machine guns, AKs, rifles, you name it, and they're all walking around the perimeter. I thought they was gonna break in, but they all got in their cars and drove away."

"What in the world were they doing?" Grave Digger asked.

"I don't know. God love it if a bunch of skinheads don't show up an hour later. They got guns, cars pulled onto our yard, and a whole mess of them walking around, looking for something, and drove off. Then the Bloods show up. It was the longest night of my life."

"In Winston-Salem?" Grave Digger said. "Wow! I never thought of that."

"Yeah. Thing was, next week there was a policeman's ball at the Denny's. I go through the whole story about the Mexicans at the store and gangs outside of my house, and I said, 'What are you doing about this stuff?'

"So the cop asked me, 'Buddy, what kind of weaponry you say these guys have?' And I told him again about the machine guns and machetes and whatnot. He pulls his sidearm out and puts it on the table and says, 'That's what I've got. That and the shotgun in my car. We could all drive down there now and start a fight, and by morning we'd be dead, and they'd still be there.'

"If I had known what it was going to be like when we moved down there, we never woulda gone."

Two men in their thirties sat across from me, Drugs and Probably Drugs. They leaned into one another and made small comments. Drugs rocked slightly in his seat. He had tattoos on his hands and face, arcane signs like a scattering of graffiti. His eyes watered. Probably Drugs was missing a tooth.

"I've walked into places like that," Drugs said. "I'd go into the projects looking for drugs. I went in one time and a girl came up to me and asked what I was doing there and I told her I was lookin' to get high, and we spent the next two days in a motel room on three hundred dollars. You can go anywhere if you act like you belong.'

"That's true," Grave Digger said. "Or if you know someone. You gotta be known."

The psychiatrist's glossy leather shoes crossed under the table. "Would you say there are a lot of predators inside the prison system as well?"

"Oh lord, yes!" Grave Digger said. "This place is full of them." Others agreed.

"What about a place like the Wall?" The psychiatrist was referring to a now-defunct correctional center that had been constructed during the Civil War.

Tucked into a corner of our imperfect circle was Murderer. Incarcerated longer than any other member of the group, he looked like a wax figure that had been left in an unconditioned warehouse during the heat of summer. He was called upon, or volunteered, whenever there were questions of antiquity. He had lived in the Wall. No one else had.

"People behaved different back then, before cameras were watching everybody. You saw things happening."

"When I got locked up," Drugs said, "in the first two weeks I heard somebody getting raped. I saw someone hang himself, and someone get jumped by three guys and beaten with a broomstick, but the worst was hearing someone being raped. That sound... I will never forget it. A man screaming like that. I was new to the system and thinking, where am I? I got locked up over half a gram of powder, and I got ten years, and I'm in a cell with a guy who killed somebody. I called home to my dad and was ready to cry, but I knew better. I told him I didn't belong with these people, murderers and rapists and child molesters, and me with half a gram of dope." His voice faltered. "I'll never forget what that sounds like. And I was lying in the cell listening to it happen."

"At Wallen's Ridge," Diabetes said, "there was a guy named Bolo who raped a bunch of people. The COs would bring 'em to him, knowing what would happen. They would laugh about it after. Certain ones, it was like a punishment. He would tell people who got in the cell with him, we can fuck or we can fight, and then I'm gonna fuck you afterwards."

"Nobody did anything to him?" Murderer said.

"This was a big dude," Diabetes said. "I'm six three, and he made me look small. He was," Diabetes squared his shoulders, "you know, a big dude. You couldn't fight him if you wanted to."

"He better not go to sleep with his door open," Murderer said. "Somebody would put an end to him."

"Nobody did," Drugs said. "People like that shouldn't be allowed to live," Murderer said.

"That was while I was there," Diabetes said. "The warden and everybody knew about it. They were giving them to him. You knew what was happening."

"What was his name?" Grave Digger asked. "Bolo, it was something like Bolo."

"When I was at Keen Mountain," Probably Drugs said, "there was a guy like that. His name wasn't Bolo, but it could have been something like that. I heard it happening."

"It does something to you," Drugs said to him, "to hear something like that." "Could a person have behaved like that at the Wall?" the psychiatrist asked. "No," Murderer said. "It wouldn't have been allowed." "He was a big guy," Diabetes said. "It doesn't matter how big he is." "Who's going to stop it?" Probably Drugs asked.

"When I first came here I tried to break up a fight," Sex Offender said. "I was walking on the rec yard and three guys jumped on one. I rushed over and tried to pull them off, and the next thing I know there are two guys pulling me back saying it's none of my business. I came from twenty years in the military to this, and it's a totally different way of looking at things. Nobody looks out for anybody. You have to watch out for yourself and keep your head down. The only people who stick together are the gangs. You can't even count on your Christian brothers to look out for you."

"A man like that Bolo is scum," Murderer said. "He shouldn't be walking around."

"It sounds like he's been in the system for years," Probably Drugs said. "So how is it the younger generation is the problem? Why hasn't anybody stopped him yet?"

"That's a good question," Murderer said. "I'm saying he should be dealt with." "Who's gonna do it?" "Somebody!"

Breaking and Entering swiveled in his seat to face Murderer. I was in between them. "I appreciate the sentiment," he said, "cuz I was one of the ones who knew better than to scream. Nobody helped me. But I appreciate the sentiment. I can't believe I've been listening to this for twenty minutes." He rose. "I've got to go."

The door closed quietly behind him. "Damn."

"Okay," the psychiatrist said, "this is probably the most emotional subject we've touched on in here. Trauma affects everyone in different ways, and I'm glad that the group was able to share so openly. I want to thank Mr. Tamil for his story, and the rest of you who shared your experiences. I'm sorry to say our time is limited, and we're going to have to wrap it up."

The group splintered into minor voices as we entered the hall that led to daylight. I overheard Probably Drugs telling Drugs that he "hated dudes like that, all talk, who wouldn't bust a grape."

I have never been a victim of sexual assault. A few penises have been whipped in my direction, but I never caught any. The thing about a man screaming remained on my mind, because I had heard it, too, several times. It was in Sussex 1, where we were locked in our cells for all but a few hours of the day. My celly made a joke about the sound, a man yelling over and over, and I took it as a joke. It occurred to me that what I was hearing could be the sound of a man being raped, but I didn't believe it was, then or after. The group had caused that memory to surface, and me to wonder.

Twenty-three hours is a long time to be locked in a cell with a predator, and every day after. You don't know what they look like, how they speak. Lions are preferable, for their honesty. Inconsistent, the predators among men may go months or years between hunts, or they may feed every night when there is opportunity. Unwritten signs and similes decipher predator from prey, and one transforms into the other when the setting suits. When I heard the man shouting in the silence of the dorm, I thought it was nothing important. Random noise is a staple of prison life. Was I hearing someone being eaten?

I believe we are defined more by what we have done than by what has been done to us. In that sense, we are more robust than those that prey upon us.

And what have I done?

My name is Robbery. It could have been something else, but that's what it is.

Second Prize, Memoir

The Week
MICHAEL JOHNSON

The body was found at approximately 3pm on a sultry Sunday afternoon, not far from the Army National Guard trailhead, by an elderly couple taking their dog out for a romp in the park. It was the animal who made the discovery, sniffing out the thirty-three-year-old male. The investigation would reveal the assailant performed his handiwork near the top of the mountain, the victim then crawling roughly a quarter mile to the bottom, finally bleeding out amidst the sand and wheatgrass covering the rifle range below

Mount Apatite is a 344-acre park, owned by the City of Auburn, Maine. Rock hunters have been poring over this area since the eighteen-hundreds, searching for tourmaline, quartz, feldspar, apatite, and garnet. For many years the Main Feldspar Company mined these minerals, while gobbling up vast quantities of mica, a mineral used to produce Formica(r), commonly found in laminated plastic products and used to produce surface finishes. Eventually the commercial digging stopped, allowing seasoned and neophyte gem-hounds alike to move in and take over. The mines filled with water and the deepest became a popular swimming hole, replete with a thirty-foot cliff to jump from. Audacious souls climbed onto the branches of sixty-foot pine trees, juxtaposed along the edge, preferring a more ostentatious display of derring-do.

The victim's car was located close to the park's main entrance, on the Garfield Road side, where the armory sits. The vehicle bore Massachusetts plates, and contained a copious amount of gay pornography. The year was 1983, long before the advent of the internet and its manifold supply of salacious material. The young man had been beaten about the head, shoulders, and upper body, suffering wounds consistent with blows from a hatchet or axe. There were defensive wounds on his hands and arms. They'd been facing each other when the attack began.

The City of Auburn purchased the land in the 1970's and in 1994 created trails for hiking, biking, cross country skiing, and snow shoeing. Snowmobiles and motorcycles saw their share of use—at one time the park hosted a lean-to belonging to a snowmobile club—until it burned down and motorized trail users were banned. Eventually the Auburn Suburban Little Leaguue relocated their fields to an area near the Garfield Road entrance, building four pristine diamonds, along with an auspicious snack bar. An illuminated Senior League Field gives older players the chance to thrill family and friends well after sundown.

Before the park took its official moniker, and even to this day I'm sure, many locals referred to the area as "the mica mines," or simply "the mines." Teenagers and young adults partied there, driving the canted, pothole-ridden dirt road to its apex. Over the years more than one stolen vehicle found its way to the bottom of the largest mine, the hole so deep it seems to reach down to earth's core. I saw a large sedan go in one night, the taillights slowly disappearing into the dark water.

I was a local, my neighborhood situated southeast of the park, a short walking distance through bordering woods. Children on my street considered the mica mines part of our locale, yoked by proximity to generations of Heath Lane progeny. My first trip came at age ten, after the purchase of a Suzuki 50cc, three-speed automatic. The perfect confluence of motorcycle and mini-bike. Once a kid from any neighborhood on the periphery of the park acquired motorized transportation, there was one destination that came to mind—the mica mines. Walking or pedaling suited many, for the mines were a place you wanted to be. You wanted to be seen there, be able to say you'd been there, to boast with authority "I go there."

Mount Apatite had a numinous quality about it. Before I ever set foot at the top, that's the feeling I held. It was sacred ground, and I wanted to stand on it. There was zero ambivalence on this topic—the mines were cool, and I was cool, for going there. Being there.

Sunday evening the rumors started. There was a large police presence on the National Guard rifle range. Not just local, but State Police as well. A body had been found. Maybe two. Someone had been shot. Stabbed. Bereft of information, people filled in the blanks in hyperbolic fashion, 24-hour news cycles not yet within our grasp. The following day's news would bring a modicum of truth to the matter. Little did I know I'd be filling in the blanks.

Monday began in the usual way. I'd graduated from Edward Little High School that Spring, and currently worked mixed shifts at Leighton's the neighborhood variety store and gas station I'd been employed at since age twelve. Local headlines gave the basics—customer gossip augmented their story—and as the sparse details seeped into my workday, my mind traveled back to a rather innocuous encounter with a customer the previous Friday night.

Afternoon shifts ran from 3-8pm except on Fridays, when they ended at 10pm. Three days ago I'd worked this shift, and at 9:55pm waited on a teenage customer decked out in full camping regalia. Most impressive was his backpack—the lightweight aluminum framed type, adorned with a sleeping bag, canteen, and other attachments.

"Where you heading so late at night with that stuff?" I asked.

"The mica mines," he answered. A resident of Lewiston, twin city to Auburn, he was getting away for a weekend of camping. Where else but the mica mines, and I gave it very little thought as he went on his way. My shift was over, my mind wandering to tomorrow's day off, and a party I would attend.

Saturday arrived, and I spent the day doing what many teenagers did before a big party back then—driving around with the host, smoking weed and gathering supplies while spreading word of our big plans. Party. Glen's house. 8pm. Parents away at camp. Awash in the evening's possibilities concerning the opposite sex, we headed into town for a load of snacks that would compliment keg beer.

It was close to 6pm when we pulled out of Garfield Road onto Minot Avenue, the intersection where Leighton's store took residence. Glancing to my right as I entered this busy four-lane highway, I spotted a hitchhiker with a large backpack. The camping kid, from work last night.

I yanked my Chevy Nova into the bicycle lane as he jogged toward us. He threw his backpack into the back seat and jumped in, expediting his entry so we could get on the move, Minot Avenue not being conducive to quick stops by the edge of the roadway.

"Hey, it's me from the store last night," I said. "Thought you were staying the weekend. You didn't make it very long."

"Oh hey," he replied." Yeah, it was cool up there, but then some gay guy started giving me a bad time, so I decided to leave early."

His comment led to the ignoble bigotry associated with the banter of teenage boys discussing homosexuality. Exacerbating the issue was our unfamiliarity with one another; that feeling you get when confined to a small space, for an indefinite period of time, with someone you don't know. Staccato cadence. Forced, banal conversation, falling far short of badinage, with a smile painted on your face. The feeling you get when chatting up a hitchhiker. I didn't know this kid—didn't even know of him. Later it would be revealed that he, too, was seventeen-years-old. In that moment, in my Chevy, with a friend and a stranger to impress, I uttered some trope regarding cutting the guy's balls off, eliciting a chorus of nervous laughter and agreement.

And just like that, it was over. Shop-and-Save loomed large in front of us, and our new acquaintance was saying he could walk the rest of the way, downtown Auburn being just across the bridge from Lewiston. And just like that, I'd forget this conversation, refocusing on my priorities of the moment—salted snacks, cold beer, and teenage girls.

*   *   *

Sunday was a beautiful day, the beginning of what would become an oppressively humid week. Glen's party fizzled just past midnight, my choice of drunken sylph proving too quick to catch. Striking out with her prompted me to sober up, driving myself home in the wee hours of the morning.

Heath Lane, the street I grew up on, is a cul-de-sac—a dead-end, the only way out being back where you came from. Unless you cut through someone's yard. This wouldn't be unusual; my own yard, and our two-acres of woodland, hosted a labyrinth of trails heading primarily toward Mount Apatite. Denizens of children from my neighborhood traipsed through these woods over the years, doing exactly that. Because we lived here. Strangers walking on our street were a rare and conspicuous sight—because Heath Lane took you nowhere.

So I was genuinely surprised when I drove past a stranger walking in the direction of my house, just after 9:30am Sunday morning. Only he wasn't a complete stranger, and I thought it uncanny how I'd seen this young camping enthusiast three times, on three consecutive days. Incredulous, I drove past, not waving or acknowledging his presence. He never looked up, his eyes locked on the ground in front of him. His appearance struck me as odd, but not overly disconcerting. I didn't know, didn't care. But on Monday, he had me curious. He'd been present too often now for me to overlook as the story gained purchase.

When the workday ended, my curiosity got the best me, and I made the call that would change his life forever, dialing up my neighbor, Auburn Detective Gerald Small. The Smalls lived six houses from me, and I was a friend to Ron and Ricky Small, the latter of whom also worked at Leighton's.

"You need to find Glen and get down here right away," exclaimed Detective Small. "How long will it take?"

"Not long," I assured him. "I'll call him now and head your way."

We arrived to find a coterie of law enforcement officials waiting to whisk us into separate offices, anxious to nail down every detail. We told our stories, mine carrying more weight as I put this young suspect near the area on three different occasions. Our part in the investigation seemingly finished, Glen and I went on our way, feeling good about giving assistance—vaunted by the fact we'd been closer than anyone to the story everyone was talking about. Nothing had been proven however, no arrest made. All we'd told was a story about a boy, on a camping trip, who'd hitched a ride after purportedly being harrassed by an adult. Mount Apatite was a big area. Almost eight miles of trails linked long-empty quarries, humongous slag piles, steep ledges, and monstrous boulders. And for all intents and purposes, a killer was still out there.

*   *   *

Mother Nature turned up the heat. By Thursday, daytime temperatures were soaring into the nineties. Glen and I were on a mission—deliver my dad's car to the post office where he worked, and recover my mom's car so she could use it that evening. I'd worked all day, and with no night-shift staring me in the face, I was considering my options for after-dark mischief.

One block from the post office we chatted away, making our party plans for that night. Every summer night was a party night, even if it meant splitting a six-pack of Mickey's Malt Liquor and a few joints. What an easy, carefree life we shared, never forced to delve much deeper than our menial-task jobs and the girls we chased, a buzz of some sort always within reach.

Stopped at the intersection of Rodman and Manley roads, Def Leppartd pouring from the speakers, we waited for traffic to clear. Rodman and Marley was a tricky intersection, traffic moving faster than the posted limit on Marley; the view partially obscured by cattails growing thick in the swampy roadside of Rodman. I edged out. Clear for a half-mile on my left; Jeep approaching fast on my right. The black Wrangler sat high on tires designed for mudding. She had the top off, roll bar prominent overhead, clipping along in excess of the suggested miles-per-hour posting. As she came closer I glanced to my left, double checking the long open view on my driver's side.

When they hit, the back end of the Jeep went up, pitching left and ejecting her from the vehicle, which landed flat on its driver's side, sliding roughly ten feet. She landed on the asphalt in front of it, dropping directly into the shards of glass that, a moment ago, made up the whole of her windshield.

Mesmerized by the garish scene unfolding in front of us, we were temporarily frozen in place. To our credit, we thawed quickly, pulling to the shoulder and jumping out.

"Check on the car," I said, pointing at the vehicle that had pulled into the intersection across from us. "I'll take care of her."

What struck me later was how quiet everything became, aside from her shrieking, a keen that would have shamed a chorus of banshees. I ran to her and she was already standing, with her arms out as if expecting a hug, in that position your hands take after unexpectedly being sprayed by water in front of a sink.

I put my right arm around her waist and she leaned into me, her cacophony of misery running at high volume. Little pieces of glass stuck in her face and arms, more in her hair. A big chunk protruded from her left hand, in the webbing between her thumb and index finger. She bled profusely, and continued screaming as I led her to an island in the middle of the intersection and sat her down. All the while I attempted to soothe her, using as cool and calm a voice as I could muster.

"You're okay." "It's going to be alright." "See, you're standing, you're walking." "You're okay." "Let's sit here, okay?" "Listen!" "Hear that?" "They're coming." The distant sound of sirens interposed on our one-sided conversation. "See that stoplight down there," I said, gesturing toward an intersection half-a-mile away. "The fire department is just around the corner."

She went silent.

"I'm going to stay right here with you until they get here," I said. "I won't leave you. Please be calm. It's going to be okay."

We sat there together, her howling reduced to whimpers and light crying. She was a lovely young woman, with blonde hair, thirty-three-years-old I would find out later, having read it in the paper. Small and fragile, someone's everything was here in my hands, counting on me to get her to the other side of this frightening circumstance; to bridge the gap between paroxysm and professional assurance.

As we huddled together on that island, the bright sun and ninety-degree temperature draping us in a shroud of intense heat, I lost track of everything. Time stopped, Glen disappeared, and the traffic crawling between the two wrecked vehicles made no sound. This traffic, with faces agape in every window, eked by only feet away, yet it seemed like she and I were all alone, far from anyone. She never said a word, and I held her close as we waited for the real heroes to arrive.

And just like that, they were there, cloistered around us, comforting and confident—but in my stupor it was all just word salad. And just like that we were separated. I stood and felt hands lifting up my shirt. A female fire fighter was saying, "Let's aget a look under there," and I realized then they thought I was in the Jeep with her. What led them to this conclusion was her blood. My teeshirt was saturated from armpit to waist, now dried and stuck to my ribcage. My jeans were darkened, and my brand new white Nikes were speckled in big, dried drops.

"I wasn't with her," I stammered. "I only stopped to help."

The police took our statements for the second time that week, and once again we were on our way, off to complete our original objective.

The people in the car were shaken, but otherwise unharmed. My island butterfly was loaded into an ambulance and carried away. That night Glen and I slept in a grove behind my house, drinking beer in front of our campfire, rehashing the day's events until we passed out.

*   *   *

Sometime after the police interviews concerning Camping Boy, Detective Small and his crew decided it would be best to check out Leighton's Store. Ricky Small had been working on the Saturday I'd picked up our camper-friend hitchhiking, so it was confirmed he'd visited the store—and used the bathroom—moments before stepping onto Minot Avenue and sticking his thumb out.

Leighton's bathroom was tiny, more like a closet with a toilet, sink, and trash can. It wasn't built for public use, but the owner had no issue with customers using it if they chose.

Garbage from the store's various trash cans was deposited in a dumpster behind the building. It was there, after a brief search, where police found the trash bag Ricky had tossed in after Camping Boy exited the store. Inside were a couple dozen blood-stained paper towels. Someone had done a thorough job of cleaning themselves up.

*   *   *

Five days after the car crash I sat in my room, listening to rock and roll on vinyl, the sound so much better than on these compact discs everyone was pushing. It was late afternoon and my workday was done—time to find a party.

"Michael, telephone!" my mom shouted, dueling with the pipes of Robert Plant.

"Hello."

"Is this Michael Johnson?" she asked.

"Yes it is."

"Hi! This is Kimberly Redding, the woman you helped in the accident last week."

My heart skipped a beat—she'd found me. She was calling to thank me, telling me she was feeling much better. No broken bones. Lots of little cuts—stitches in her left hand. Very lucky to have walked away from it, they'd told her. Very luck to have me, she said, thanking me again and again. Nonplussed, all I could say was "You're welcome," and "No problem."

"Michael, how old are you?"

"Seventeen," I said, adding that I'd just graduated in June.

"Seventeen! My God, you're so young!"

And just like that she was gone, thanking me once more, and blessing me as she moved from living entity to distant memory, to be revived only in moments of drunken braggodocio, or those times when friends compare iconic events from their past. On cardgame and movie nights, when the conversation turns on a flashback, and someone says "I remember the time..."

Years after drugs and alcohol stole my college education, long past the time bipolar disorder and addiction altered my path, even after I'd gone to prison for the first time, I never forgot Kimberly Redding and that hot summer day. A day when someone had a reason to thank me for helping them when they were scared and hurt. The type of help I wish I'd had when my life crashed and flipped over onto its side, dumping me into the roadway alone.

People called me and Glen heroes for the things we did that week, but I didn't feel like one, the gravity of the events reaching far beyond my teenage pay scale. No, they were just things anyone would have done, should they ever walk in these same shoes. Besides, wasn't life full of these exciting moments, something fresh and novel every day, now that we were adults?

Heroes? Maybe. Probably not. Either way, we had a lot more to learn about life.

*   *   *

In the Fall of 1984 I returned home from class one day to find visitors waiting. Two Maine State Police detectives sat in our kitchen while my mom busied herself with laundry and dishes.

They had a photo line-up, and wanted to know if I could pick Camping Boy out of a group of six men: I wasn't sure. It had been so long since I'd seen him—and I hadn't spent much time looking at his face. I sat at the kitchen table with them for more than an hour, vacillating between choices, trepidation creeping in every time I wanted to commit.

"Take your time," one of them said. "We're in no hurry." And they didn't seem to be, remaining calm and stoic throughout, impervious to my concerns that I would "wreck their whole case."

"That's him," I said finally, as I pointed to a young man with dark, wavey hair.

"Are you sure?" the other asked.

"Yes, I'm sure."

Without a hint of elation, or disappointment, they thanked me for my time, gathered their belongings and went on their way. I never saw them again. Days later I was visiting the Small's, talking to their dad about the case, telling him I was afraid I'd botched the identification of their suspect.

"Well, Mike," he said, "I'm not supposed to tell you this, so don't repeat it. You got him."

Of course, this was good news. A killer caught meant justice would be served. A family would find closure. As I smiled and thanked Detective Small for telling me, one might have believed those were the thoughts I was having—but I wasn't. Any joy I felt for having helped the police was fleeting, just as the happiness I found in anything now was short lived.

As Camping Boy was making his way to prison, I was embarking on a journey of mental illness, addiction and abject failure, my successes fewer and farther between from this point on. In twenty years I'd been on my way to prison, facing the same fears he must have felt as a teenager.

Camping Boy. I didn't even know his name; I may have heard it once, but have no memory of it now. Under different circumstances perhaps we would have known each other, been friends—we were both seventeen. That week. That week where we each wore the blood of another human, drenched in it for totally different reasons. Maybe we would have drank beer, smoked joints, chased girls, and slept in the grove behind my house.

But we didn't.

And just like that, the week that felt as though it would never end, finally did.

Round One
RAYLAN GILFORD

ROUND 1

I landed at Danville Correctional Center in the winter of 2012. I placed all of my property into a rolling cart and headed towards Three House, B Wing, Upper Tier, Cell 71. When I made it to the unit, Officer Friendly slid me a key on top of a piece of paper with his index finger pointing to a specific section, and said, "Sign here."

"What's that for? You trying to set me up?" I respond, refusing to take the key.

Officer Friendly laughs in my face. And said, "No, I am not trying to set you up, sir; every inmate receives a key to his cell."

"I ain't going!"

He laughs even louder then tosses the key in my direction, forcing me to catch it midair.

"Now sign here please."

I hesitantly sign the paper as Officer Friendly orally regurgitates what is written above the X mark for my signature.

"If you lose the key it is going to cost you $20 to replace it. NEXT!"

Unlike at Menard Correctional Center, when I stepped on B Wing there wasn't any anger, malice, rage, or violence floating in the atmosphere. Not feeling the negative tension that I normally felt upon entering a new facility really scared the shit out of me. So much so, that my fight or flight mechanism got stuck on red alert and I couldn't turn it off. My demeanor must have unmasked the anxiety, because every person I passed looked at me like I was crazier than two motherfuckers. And those suspicious stares only sent my fear levels into the stratosphere. It's amazing what you'll adapt to in prison and accept as normal when it is actually the apex of abnormality. I silently prayed.

Oh GOD, please protect me 'cause I don't know what is about to happen.

Allah heard my prayer. I was blessed to be housed with this smooth young brother from Decatur named Fat Man, but he wasn't fat at all. Go figure. As I laid in the top bunk, he walked back and forth in our little abode, sharing the particulars of this medium security prison. He moved with such style and grace, and spoke from a position of power like a commercialized Billy D. Williams who just finished off a tall can of Colt 45. I ain't gonna' stunt, he was cooler than two anorexic lovers in an air conditioned room with the ceiling fan on and I admired his swag.

Every single time that I've been caged in with a new cellmate it takes about two or three weeks to pass before I get to see the "real him." Eighteen years into a thirty-two and a half year bid, I finally ran into the exception to that rule. The way Fat Man introduced himself was the way he continued to be. And six months easily breezed by before he laid the KABOOM!

"Sheed, I'm finta' move in the cell with one of my homies from D Town."

"Come on, man," I joylessly let out.

"Me and him ran the streets together and I wanna hang out with him before I go to the crib."

How could I argue with that? So I feebly took a swing at their brotherhood.

"Man you gonna' go down there, get in trouble, and jag your out date."

"You know I ain't on that, and if he is then that's on him, 'cause ain't no nigga finta' stop me from getting to my baby boy!"

I felt he truly meant that last statement because in the one hundred and eighty three days that we peacefully lived together, that was the first time that he had ever raised his voice.

Seven days later Fat Man moved out and like clockwork Mr. JD dragged right on in. JD was short, pudgy, with a bigass head like a retarded Rottweiler. And this nigga had the nerve to have a lil' Kobe Bryant afro on the top of that worn-out medicine ball. Where do these niggas come from?

"What's up man, my name Rasheed," I said, as I helped him slide his property boxes into the cell.

"They call me JD," he expressed with a smile.

I was about to relax but for some reason his smile looked fake, like he was forcing it upon his face. Right there was an immediate red flag because he was being weird for no reason at all.

BBBeeeeppp! Off sides, on the defense, ten yard penalty, repeat first down.

But at the same time I had to pick up the flag because what if he was just as afraid of living in a cell with me, as I was of being trapped in a cage with him?

BBBeeeeppp! Bad call, the initial ruling on the field stands, still first down.

Anyway, he had all of his electronics, a box full of food, and he was from the Southside of Chicago. Check, check, and more positive checks. He was a taxi driver by trade, could hold a conversation, and think a little bit. JD caught me up on all the latest hood shit and even shared a few of those sexually-comedic taxi driving tall tales.

So I began to relax, thinking, I done' came up again.

Oh, how I was so fracking wrong. The very first day, later that evening, during the middle of one of our many conversations, he turned his back to me, took a piss in the toilet, wiped the metal seat with a rolled up wad of tissue paper, and flushed. But he didn't wash his fucking hands, and he continued to talk like he didn't just touch his man meat.

Relax. I wasn't watching him while he was pissing. I caught all of that with my peripheral vision. I'm in a 7' by 10' two-man cell, so his derriere was literally 3' away from my face. Honestly, at that distance, if he were to fart, I would smell his ass before he would, and maybe even taste it a little.

Kids, stay out of prison if you don't like the taste and smell of another man's ass. And if you do, sign up, and you will never be disappointed at the variety of shit smells that the Prison Industrial Complex has in store for you.

Please let this be a mistake, I thought before I went into my verbal Judo mode.

"Hey JD, I'm not trying to be nosy or disrespectful but I noticed you took a piss, but you didn't wash your hands."

"Yeah you saw right," he standoffishly responded.

"Why wouldn't you wash your hands when you just touched your SWILLER?"

"I don't touch my dick when I piss."

"What?!"

I sort of chuckled, not because what he voiced was funny. I laughed because I couldn't believe what he just said to me. This nigga talking like he got an autonomous fire-hose dick. How do you respond to something like that? "I don't touch my dick when I piss."

I decided to move past the dick touching and attack from the pissy tissue angle.

"What about when you wipe urine off the toilet seat with the tissue paper? Don't you think you need to wash your hands then?"

"Naw, 'cause I don't get no piss on the seat," he answered with a smirk.

Is this nigga serious or is he fucking with me? Becoming annoyed, I retorted, "So why wipe the toilet seat at all if you piss like a God?"

"That's for the backlash of toilet water that pops out from the force of my piss," he stated matter of factly.

"Well, why don't you clean the toilet water from your hands then?"

"I use enough tissue when I wipe, so the toilet water never touch my fingers."

He had me right there and it all made sense, especially in crazy language. I initially thought I had a Chi-town Fat Man in the cell with me, but he turned out to be just another nasty motherfucker. So I fell all the way back after that fruitful toiletry discussion.

Danville Correctional Center is a laid back medium security prison. I'm not advocating police'ism in any sense, but in the interest of truth, it's safe to say that the abundance of good cop'ers in Danville far outweigh the totality of cranks.

Medium security prison means extra-extra privileges and even more time outside of your cell to move around and sniff some fresh air. In addition to yard and gym time, everyday, we get two separate Dayroom Times, one in the AM and the other in the PM, lasting about an hour and a half, respectively.

The Dayroom is a 25' by 125' space that has on the front end six strategically placed old school phone booths made of thinly meshed metal minus the front door with Plexiglas that Clark Kent would need to change into Superman. Furthermore, up front on the upper and lower tier in plain view of the observation pod, is a shower section with two individual shower heads. A plastic shower curtain hangs about 4' in the air and ends about 2' from the ground. There is just enough plastic to cover your sex organs from the viewing observation officer. But most importantly, the height and length of the plastic hinders one behavior and equally keeps an inmate from being raped or sexually abused. On the back end of the wing are four spaciously placed tables, with four connecting backless McDonald's seats, all of which are bolted to the floor. If you haven't figured it out by now, this in-house recreational area is spacious enough for fifty men to use the phone, take showers, socialize, play card games, chess, dominoes, scrabble, or whatever.

What I love the most about Dayroom Time is the mere fact that I can take a shit now, in the cell, without the company of my roommate. He can pop out and go about his business. Then, I can sit butt naked on the commode with one dirty sock on and do the damn thang.

It's the little things, baby, the little things.

Three weeks passed with Mr. Pissy Hands. So in order to stay healthy, rest my worrying mind, and keep the peace, I would soap up the sink, light switch, or any other communal area before usage. Yeah, I went through a lot of soap but at least I got to shower twice a day if I wanted, as opposed to showering only twice a week like at Menard maximum security prison. Fuck this nasty-ass creep; I ain't trying to go backwards.

One day we got served some half-cooked baked chicken for lunch. My mind told me not to eat the shit. But my appetite got the better of me. Take note, I said it here first, the chicken stereotype is true: All black folks love chicken. Me even more so because I ate it at the risk of salmonella poisoning. In defense of my people, there ain't nothing strange surrounding the reasons why "WE" love chicken so. On top of it being a delicious treat, we fancy yard-bird because we grew up eating it. And why are we orientated towards poultry? Chicken is one of the least expensive foods on the market. And any right-minded person will tell you that a nice percentage of African Americans are in bad shape financially. So, when you're poor, the more bang that you can get out of your buck is always a plus. Hence, the climb in poultry sales. Now, why are "WE" as a people in such poor financial health? You can blame slavery, institutional racism, marginalization, or the white, capitalistic, patriarchal society (America) ... Pick one.

Equally, white people love eating fried chicken just as much as black people. When I worked in Downtown Chicago I used to see white folks in those duel restaurants and food courts waiting for some Kentucky Fried Chicken. The KFC lines were always around the corner and out the door. A brother couldn't get any chicken downtown with only an hour lunch break.

"Welcome to McDonalds! May I take your order please?"

"Ummm... Yeah... let me get a Big Mac and a..." You white motherfuckers love some chicken too, and rightly so; it's inexpensive and delicious.

Well anyway, that half cooked chicken gave me the bubble guts for real. So I was forced to shit on three different occasions with JD in the cell. It's weird defecating in a pantry sized room with another man. Even though we're allowed to hang a sheet for privacy, it still feels like I'm taking a dump in a grammar school restroom with a missing stall door, and my cellmate is sitting on the bathroom sink across from me, watching me shit. Yeah, that's one way to describe it. After the third Black Hawk Down, I soaped my hands, and laid down in the fetal position because my stomach was still killing me.

"Rasheed, you good?" JD said.

"Naw man, that chicken fucked me up. The system ain't shit."

JD laughed and I followed suit because the system ain't force me to eat that paleolithic chicken.

"They got me too," JD shared as he jumped off the top bunk and hung his sheet to defecate.

About fifteen minutes passed before JD's exorcism was complete. He got up, removed the sheet, and jumped straight in his bed without washing his motherfucking hands. OH HELL NO! Fuck verbal Judo, I went straight into attack mode.

"JD why you ain't wash your hands and you just got through taking a shit?!"

"Cause my fingers don't touch my asshole, the tissue do."

"WHAT?!"

"I'm thirty-two years old; I know how to wipe my ass without getting shit on my fingers!"

"What about when you stick your hand in the toilet to wipe? Don't you think the impurities on the inside and the splashing toilet water needs to be washed off?!"

"Naw, I'm good on that too 'cause I lift my ass high enough to where my hand never lands inside the toilet."

Now I was going crazy 'cause the shit he's saying is starting to make sense to me. Then I heard my mom's voice inside my head like the Jedi Master Obi Wan Kenobi would pop up in Luke Skywalker's mind whenever he doubted himself.

You ain't crazy, that nasty motherfucker CRAZY!

So I fought on.

"Why you scared to clean your hands?!"

"I ain't scared. That's just a waste of soap."

"HERE!" I said, attempting to pass him a fresh bar of Irish Spring

"Naw, you can keep that. If I ain't gonna' waste mine then why would I waste yours?"

I had to take a seat, collect my thoughts, and critically analyze this whole shitty situation before I DDT'ed this motherfucker.

Anger is not working and I definitely can't beat this nigga ass because he gone' have shit residue everywhere. Then they gonna' ship me out this sweet-ass joint faster than Usain Bolt running after an Olympic gold metal. I got a key to my cell... I got a key to my cell... I got a key to my cell... So what can I do? Hopefully my sense of humor can get me out of this one.

I stood up, looked him straight in his eyes and said,

"JD, I been locked up for eighteen years straight and I have never indulged in any homosexual activities. Whether you get shit on your fingers or not, if you don't wash your hands after you defecate then touch the water buttons or light switch, in my mind your smearing dookie everywhere. Then if I come behind you and press the same buttons or hit the light, I feel like my hand is touching the bitter sweet softness of your asshole. I been locked up a long time and I can only resist for so long. Please Don't Make A Fag Out Of Me," I said ending with my hands together in the prayer position.

JD fell out laughing and I kept going.

"Im'a need you to wash your hands after you piss too, 'cause if you don't and I touch what you touch, I feel like I'm JAGGING YOUR DICK."

He laughed even louder and I kept chopping away at his insanity with my jokes.

"What do you call a hand that's on your Swiller that you don't know?"

"A hand job!" he barked out in the midst of his laughter.

"Naw, that's called a sneaky motherfucker. Nigga, I don't want to know you intimately and I definitely don't wanna receive a sneaky motherfucker, so wash your HANDS!"

I laughed along with him because I finally got through to this crazy motherfucker. Some people may say that JD is just trifling, but not crazy, and I get that. In defense of my position, you got to be crazy if you think you can take a shit, and not wash your hands, smearing fecal matter everywhere. Even the teachers of Socrates, the Pre-Socratics from ancient Kemet and Kush say, and I'm paraphrasing, "If you don't wash your hands after releasing body waste than you are a crazy motherfucker." And I tend to agree.

Real talk, by us being creatures of habit, I believe he only washed his hands when I was in his presence. I bet you, whenever I would leave the cell, he would take a 40oz malt liquor piss or a Macho Man Randy Savage shit and purposely abstain from washing his hands to spite me. Then he'd touch my TV buttons, fan, tape player, and pillow case just because he could. PRISON SUCKS!!!

WHAT WOULD YOU DO IF YOU WERE ME?

ROUND 2

When you're on the precarious road of life, whether you're in the free world or in prison, you pick up real friends along the way and discard the rest.

One of my homeboyz told me, "Sheed you got to be careful in them lil' camps 'cause the lower level you go, the more creeped-out them niggas be."

I laughed, but in time I learned that it wasn't anything funny to be taken from his forewarning.

Around the end of September 2015 at Danville, during the second week in Ramadan, I received a new cellmate. He was a special delivery from Lawrenceville Correctional Center. My prior roomie got a job with the Dietary Department so he happily moved to the workers' deck. All the things that I had encountered during my extensive incarceration could never have prepared me for this moment. A 5' 11", mid-40s, Blackman with an angry demeanor, beer belly, and short ass arms stood in the doorway.

"How you doing, Bra', my name Rasheed," I said sticking out my fist.

"Yea, I'm K-Dub," he aggressively replied, refusing to give me some dap.

I didn't take his response personally. He could have been having a bad day. Plus, I was in the thick of Ramadan, so my emotions could have been at an all-time high. Ramadan is the ninth month of the Islamic calendar. Around this time of the year Muslims all over the world abstain from food and drink from sunrise till sunset. In addition, we also refrain from lying, cursing, backbiting, lusting, or anything else displeasing to Allah. Twenty nine to thirty days of this abstinence has you "Open" mentally, spiritually, physically, emotionally, sexually, and intellectually in ways you could never have imagined. This "Openness" is hard to explain. So Im'a just leave it there and say, fast during the month of Ramadan a day or two, maybe more, and you'll see first hand what I'm talking about.

"You want me to help you with your stuff?"

"No."

So I slid on the bunk and kept reading my Holy Quran. Several hours of uncomfortable silence passed before we spoke again.

"Rasheed, can I get these three pegs over here? 'Cause I don't want my stuff all by the door."

"Yea, just switch'em around."

"Naw, I don't want to touch your shit. I'll just wait till you move it."

"Man, gone' move that stuff."

"I can wait until you get a chance to move it."

Drilled into the wall, in every cell, next to the door about eye level, is a wooden coat rack with six reasonably spaced four-inch timber pegs extending out to hang clothing. His willingness to wait on me was a total farce because he stood in the middle staring at the coat rack. And the tone he used was prison lingo for, was "Nigga, hurry up and move your shit so I can get situated."

So I jumped on up and shifted my clothing to the far end of the rack.

What did you get out of that little conversation that K-Dub and I just had? Go ahead. Take a moment, and think about it. Read it again if you have too, because there is a lot being said about his character with that little back and forth.

K-Dub just told me in so many words that he's paranoid and extremely territorial. Moreover, he clearly stated in no uncertain terms that while we're living together, he ain't gonna' touch my "shit" and I better not touch his "shit." Understand?

The more we converse, the more I'll be able to figure him out, and move accordingly so we can coexist within this little space. I've had plenty of angry and territorial cellmates. The initial formula for survival is the same minus a few underlying personality adjustments here and there:

#1) I'll never engage or start a conversation with him. Angry people say angry shit and I'm hanging onto my happiness by a thread. I don't need his words pulling at that string.

#2) I'll never touch his property, unless given permission, which is extremely hard to do when you have two grown men crammed into a custom made panic room for a malnourished midget.

#3) I'll never take his angry demeanor or territoriality personal. He got a right to be mad; he was judicially kidnapped from his loved ones and snatched away from all the sweet-old liberties of American life. You'd be pissed too.

Moreover, his territorial issues could have stemmed from cellmates that came before me. Anyone of them could have broken an electronic of his or stole some of his property. So if he wants to put police tape around his penitentiary possessions for protection, so be it. I understand.

The few times that he spoke to me after the coat rack incident were all negative, laden with expletives, and he often highlighted the fact that he had fifteen more years of incarceration to complete before being released. His energy-draining rants were a slick way of saying, "I'm a Mad, Bad, Motherfucker and I ain't got shit to lose."

I heard him loud and clear. Normally, to put someone like this in their place, I would fight fire with fire and share my penitentiary pedigree with something like, "Nigga that ain't shit, I done' over fifteen years, and a large percentage of that time was spent in THE PIT."

The Pit is what we call Menard's Maximum Security Prison for short. Why? Someone took a heap of dynamite and blew a 90' foot hole into the ground the size of a small town and built a penal institution inside that space. Then they filled the joint with 3,000 of Illinois's convicted and extremely dangerous gang chiefs, murderers, rapists, drug dealers, and all around low life bastards, like The Pit of Hell/Hades spoken of so freely in the Holy Bible for unrepentant sinners.

For the first time in a long time I chose not to share my incarcerated background. I was too busy enjoying the blessed month of Ramadan to engage in any psychological cell games. My unwillingness to utilize a successful negative formula to combat his negativity and turn this whole situation semi-positive would come back later on and bite me in the ass.

My penitentiary super-jerk meter is top shelf. So whenever I come in contact with a hateful motherfucker, I can just feel the loathing radiating up off of his presence. And the tension in the cell with this crank reeked of such vileness for three days straight, but it felt more like three weeks.

Day four, dinner tray in hand, I came back to the cell cute as a button after indulging in engageful conversations and Congregational Salat. I hadn't eaten in about fifteen hours. So you know I was more than ready to wolf down a double burger with fries, and fat-boyish'ly enjoy a big chunk of white cake with chocolate icing heavily smeared on top. Black on white baby!

One of the many joys of Ramadan is the breaking of the fast. I've never known food to smell or taste so good. After fasting, you could be eating a plain Saltine cracker and get to smacking your lips like, "Is this paprika I taste?"

Anyway, I opened the cell door and was immediately smacked in the face with the smell of diesel fuel, like I just Trolloped into an overbooked diesel-automotive mechanics shop. What The Fuck Is That?! sounds off in my mind. Instantly my head began to hurt as I looked for the cause of such foulness. I found nothing, so I'm forced to violate one of my rules of survival with an angry nigga.

"K-Dub, what's that smell?"

"What smell?"

"Come on man."

"Oh, that's my fan."

"Why it's blowing out that smell?"

"It needed some oil. I ain't have none so I used hair grease!" he angrily retorted as if he was done with my line of questioning.

At that point I didn't care how he felt 'cause he done fucked up my whole meal and he got my head hurting.

"Why would you use hair grease? Better yet, why do you think your fan needs any oil at all? Did you read the instructions when you brought it?"

His silence revealed his stupidity and lack of concern for my questions.

"You got the whole cell stanking. You plan on cleaning your fan anytime soon?"

K-Dub exhales loud and hard like I'm the problem, then says, "It ain't bothering me!"

I think to myself, ain't that a bitch, I know that smell fucking with him but he know it's affecting me more because I'm fasting. And just when I was about to go HAM my Taqwa steps in. Rasheed it's Ramadan, be the bigger man, and wash the fan.

"You mind if I wash it then, 'cause that smell got my head hurting?"

"If you break my fan, you gone' buy me a new one!" he threateningly declared.

I almost said, "Nigga, I'm a break your ass in here if you keep talking tuff!"

But it was Ramadan, Ramadan, Ramadan. So I humbled myself further.

"If I break it while cleaning, I'll pay for a new one."

"Go head then, nigga," he Scarface' ly answered.

I laughed and shook my head because I was starting to think that this creep's taking my meekness for weakness. Meekness is never weakness; it's strength under control, and I'm as strong as they come.

When I finished cleaning his fan I plugged it up, turned it on, and K-Dub smiled like an evil villain. Then sarcastically said, "You did a good job, its blowing better than the first day I brought it."

My primary thought at his taunting... did he do this on purpose, knowing I was fasting so I would have to clean his fan or feel sick? Affirmative, because his grease-laden fan was full of dust.

Like when the turtle raced the hare, six more days crawled by before we spoke again. It was lunchtime and I popped out to holler at Big Trav before he left for chow. In the middle of our conversation K-Dub rudely interrupted,

"Rasheed Dump The Garbage!"

Quick side note: In prison, there's penitentiary etiquette about everything. For example, if two people are talking and you need to holler at one of them, you must say "excuse me" before you interrupt their conversation. You just can't bust in and start talking like what you have to say is more important than their discussion. Actions like that are considered disrespectful and a quick way to get your ass kicked.

Me and Big Trav glanced K-Dub's way and went right back to talking like he never existed. While kicking the boboes, I happened to notice with my peripheral vision that K-Dub went in and out of the cell two more times before the line left for chow.

Every cell has a small 1′ by 1′ by 1′ plastic rectangular garbage receptacle. When I came into the cell and looked into the trash can, it was less than half way full. Thinking out loud, "This nigga trippin'. Ain't no garbage even in there. And why he ain't dump it himself?"

I went back to my favorite episode of Seinfeld, the one where they all bet money to see who could go the longest without masturbating, and I laughed away until the lunch line returned.

"Rasheed, why you ain't dump that garbage?"

"What's wrong with your hands?" I shoot-back and K-Dub snatched up the trash can and dumped it into a larger wastebasket outside the cell.

"I don't like a full garbage can cause that's gone bring bugs!" K-Dub yelled as he slammed the empty can to the floor.

"Man it wasn't hardly no garbage in there!" I expressed with a mug on my face.

"It's still gonna' bring bugs!"

"Look here man, you walked in and out this cell on two different occasions after you rudely interrupted my conversation. Why you ain't dump the garbage then, since you're so concerned about bugs?"

"Ummm...Ahhh... I—"

"Hold on, Saturday when I soaped up the walls and cleaned the floor I didn't ask you to help me. Did I?" Not waiting for an answer I continued,

"So why you need me to help you dump some garbage?"

He just found out that I'm intense with common sense.

"I'm just trying to keep bugs out our cell," he rightfully put forth.

"Where is all these bugs you keep talking about anyway? Man you trippin'. Don't involve me in that!"

Right then I realized I was angry. I quickly turned down so I wouldn't knowingly violate my fast. About thirty minutes passed and K-Dub jumped out of the bunk and did something that caught me totally off guard.

"Rasheed, I apologize about the garbage. You right I was trippin' 'cause you ain't ask me to clean up nothing around here."

"It's cool man. Ain't no big thang."

His apology felt sincere as he looked me in the eyes for the very first time. Honestly, I thought we'd be alright after that incident.

Four more days passed before our next confrontation. I popped out the cell to empty a full wastebasket like any normal minded person would do. I left the cell door open because the communal trash can is literally five pistol dueling paces away. When I returned moments later I was greeted by that old familiar K-Dub scowl.

"Rasheed, why you keep leaving that door open?!"

"What's wrong now?"

"You keep leaving the door open! What if somebody ran up in here on me while I was getting dressed?!"

"Run in on you? Man, ain't nobody finta' run in on you, you in Danville not Statesville!"

"That don't mean shit. I'm still in prison!"

Feeling my anger boil during the blessed month of Ramadan, I chose to go into a 402 Conference.

"So what you want me to do? Lock the door whenever I leave the cell even if I'm taking a few steps to the garbage?"

"YEAH!!"

"Alright, it won't happen again." Alhamdulillah, I bowed out gracefully.

This nigga acting like he some supreme hood serial killer that everybody's trying to murder to earn their stripes. I bet you this mark was a scary ass crack-head or a sneaky ass dope-fiend in the world, and after being drug-free for a while because of incarceration, all of a sudden he's a lean mean killing machine. Lucky number thirteen is what I said in my head as I counted the number of days that I've been housed with this crank. Lucky #13.

The sun rose and set two more times, drama free, before we bumped heads again. It was afternoon Dayroom Time. I patiently waited for K-Dub to pop out then I began making the proper preparations to take a nice dump. First, I slid a piece of paper in the door. This piece of paper is the universal penitentiary sign that says to all those around, I'm Busy, Do Not Disturb!

Next, I lined the cold, hard metal seat with toilet tissue, got butt ass naked, put on my lucky sock, and jumped on the motorcycle. I was smack dab in the middle of shitting like a dog when I hear K-Dub screaming my name at the top of his lungs from the Dayroom.

"Rasheed! Rasheed!! Rasheed!!! You Through Yet?!!!!?"

I think out loud, "Is this nigga crazy? I know he see the sign in the door. Why he hollering my name like that?"

I looked at my timepiece. Ain't nothing but five minutes then went by. Fuck him, he can holler until his throat box burst for all I care. And holler he did, over and over again.

"Rasheed!! What's taking so long?!!!"

About five more minutes passed before I was done. As I calmly reached back to wipe my ass, I saw this nigga's face in the chuckhole, staring at me.

A chuckhole is like an institutional key hole that can be utilized from both sides of the door. It's an eye level, semi-grated metal square that's used by the correctional officers to count and observe an inmate's behavior.

When our eyes locked, he mugged up then walked away like I done fucked up his day. I screamed in my head, Is this nigga a fag?! I'm checking this creep as soon as I get through.

I wiped my ass, washed my hands, got dressed, removed the sign then pushed the door all the way open. The month of Ramadan had ended the day before so I was more than ready to beat his ass for today's stunt and for his attitude in times gone by.

He came in and slammed the door behind him. BOOM! His back was all hunched up, like a silverback gorilla with some little ass arms. I wasn't impressed or scared in the least.

"Man why you hollering my name like you crazy while I'm on the shitter?!"

"My bad, I thought you had the sign in the door for no reason."

"Naw, fuck...my bad. Why you hollering my name like you crazy?!"

By that being the first time he ever heard me drop an "F bomb," his eyes got big, posture straighten up, and his demeanor and tone softened.

"I done had cellies that keep the sign in the door for hours and when I looked in, they ain't doing nothing but watching TV."

"Hours! Nigga the sign was in the door about five minutes before you started acting crazy!"

He just stood there looking stupid.

Real talk, right then and there I wanted to steal on his ass. But the Holy Month had just ended and the same humility I displayed during Ramadan should be held throughout the entire year. So I turned down and decided to use my charisma to open his eyes.

"K-Dub have I ever done anything in this cell that would lead you to believe that I would purposely keep the sign in the door?"

"No."

"So why did you think I'd be on something like that?"

"You might of forgot it."

"You didn't give me a chance to forget, it was only in there five minutes!"

He was still trying to justify this creep shit. So it was clear that my charisma wasn't working. Inspired by my favorite Seinfeld episode I warped into comedy mode.

"Look at it like this bra', what if I was in here masturbating and about to buss the best nut ever then you get to calling my name? I know you don't want me thinking about you at the POINT-OF-NO-RETURN," I said, emphasizing the last four words.

He smiled for the first time, started laughing then said,

"Alright Rasheed you win, as long as that sign is in the door, you ain't gonna' hear nothing from me."

"That's all I ask."

"Can I ask you a question?"

"Shoot."

"Why was you naked on the toilet with one sock on?"

"Why was you looking at me? You wasn't even supposed to see that!" And we laughed some more.

Two dog days later, I was knocked out asleep on the left side of my body, facing the wall with a sheet pulled completely over my head.

I was slightly awakened by the sensation of something tugging at the sheet down by my boxer shorts. I lay still, fully awake, not sure if I was dreaming or if somebody had actually touched me. A few moments later I feel someone pulling at my boxer shorts again. I quickly removed the sheet from over my head and sat up. I saw K-Dub arm move to the top bunk as if he was reaching for something upon his bed. Although I was in my full right to go berserk without question, all I wanted to know was, why? No anger, no malice, only WHY?

"Man, why was you tugging on my sheet down by my boxer shorts?"

"Oh, my bad. My knee must of hit you when I was reaching for my ID."

"Man I know the difference between a push and a pull, why was you touching me while I was sleep?"

"Motherfucker, I told you that was my knee! Wasn't nobody touching you!!!" he said screaming loud as ever.

"I don't know what you getting loud fo'. I'm just trying to get some clarity about this situation."

"Fuck clarity. You accusing me of something I ain't do!"

"Alright man, I'm gone from the situation; PLEASE stop talking to me."

K-Dub never lowered his tone and he kept cussing and fussing like he was checking me. I looked at my watch; it was 4:16 am. I put my gym shorts on stepped into my shower shoes and washed my face. K-Dub was fully dressed because he had an early morning call pass to the Health Care Unit. The more I thought about what just took place, the more my blood boiled, and the loudness of his voice faded into the background.

Was this nigga just feeling on me like I was a bitch or something !?

Then flashbacks of all of our run-in's rapidly shot through my mind like a sexual assault victim on a Lifetime Channel movie special: the coat rack and garbage can incident, me washing his fan, his predatory eyes upon my ass while I was defecating, and now him touching on me.

The cell door popped open as I put my face towel away. K-Dub walked out and slammed the room door hard as hell. BOOM!!!!

That was it; I couldn't hold back any longer. Fuck waiting until the 7:00am shift change to holler at a lieutenant to get moved. Fuck this sweet-ass joint. Fuck everything. It's time for me to speak in a language that I know he would understand: VIOLENCE!

So I moved swiftly to the chuckhole and hollered out, "What that supposed to mean?!"

K-Dub yelled back, "Pop the door and I'll show you!!!!"

I pushed the cell door button but it did not open. Right then and there time slowed down even though it was moving hella-fast. I looked down and realized that I didn't have my gym shoes on as K-Dub slid his key into the keyhole.

Fuck! No time to slide' em on now, I gotta go barefoot, I thought in my head as I kicked my shower shoes off and to the side.

When K-Dub turned his key, the door popped, and he snatched it open with his left hand then cocked his right hand back in an attempt to punch me in my eye.

K-Dub had an evil ass look on his face similar to Freddy Kruger from The Nightmare on Elm Street when his razor-sharp-knifed-glove is up in the air and he's about to swing down upon a cornered teenage victim.

Quick side note: I wrestled for Chicago Vocational High School and I went Down-State my Junior year. Also, over the years of my incarceration I've learned how to properly defend myself. Yes, I am a practitioner of "The Sweet Science." Then, when you sprinkle on top of that my hood/penitentiary rage, I'm kind of like Liam Neeson from the movie Taken, "I have a particular set of skills." No bullshit! Smile.

Anyway, his right hand was cocked back and I went straight up the middle with an upper cut. BAM!! His evil ass demeanor was quickly replaced by one of surprise and his knifed-gloved/right hand disappeared from sight. After that everything else was textbook. Like Coach Howell would say, "Throw punches with a purpose." And that I did.

I went straight to his head; jab, right hand, left uppercut, right hook, hook, and hook. I landed about eleven blows of an eighteen punch combination, and this nigga ain't drop yet. He recovered and caught me with a one-two, but there wasn't much on it. The first one landed over my right eye and I semi-slipped the second punch because it only grazed the top of my head. I stepped back on an angle and K-Dub smiled as if to say, "Yea nigga, I'm still here!"

I doubled up the jab and when he backed into a dayroom table I threw the right hand. It landed on his chest, from there I grabbed his neck and used my other hand to grab his outer right thigh and slammed him to the floor. BOOM! Single leg takedown, Coach Howell would have been proud.

When we hit the floor my hood/penitentiary rage took over and I slammed about four Donkey Kong hammer fists upon his face, before K-Dub finally broke and started screaming for mercy.

"Alright Rasheed that's enough!!!!"

"I'm a man. Fuck you touching me for while I'm sleep? YOU CREEP!!!" I yelled as a correctional officer football tackled me up off of him.

After being blindsided, I turned straight off as if a fighting bell had ended the round.

"Hey, officer, can I get dressed?"

"Sure," he responded with a strange look on his face, as we both rose from the ground.

I can only assume that he was trying to figure out how I went from Spartacus to Mr. Rogers all within a blink of an eye. I wanted to tell him that's just one difference between being trained and untrained; you tense when you throw and relax when you ain't.

I was cuffed up, taken to the Health Care Unit, then segregation.

The only good thing about this whole situation of being housed with a creep is that as long as I'm in Danville Correctional Center I'll never have to fight again. Why? My reputation will precede me. Between me and you, I don't like being violent. I'm only brave when I have to be, but some niggas in prison, all they seem to understand is brutality.

WHAT WOULD YOU DO IF YOU WERE ME?

Fielding Dawson Prize, Memoir

Poker Face
HEATHER C. JARVIS

A million different emotions flooded through me like a hurricane of despair and euphoria. It was Family Day at the Ohio Reformatory for Women. The day was drawing to an end.

How do you look your father in the eyes, the person who raised you, knowing it is the last time you will ever see him? It's terrifyingly tragic.

The day went too fast, filled with the chaos of sticky-faced children who ate way too much candy from the pinnate running every which way between activities. The face painting station was packed with children expectantly wanting Spiderman or butterfly faces. The sounds of children and line dancing music filled the gym. The bowling pins were being trampled like grass at a yard sale by young ones too little to even put their fingers in a ball correctly. Mothers gleefully chased after them, even if it was just for a day.

Unlike them, that day was all I had.

Family Day was the only chance I had to look in my father's eyes. To feel his soft weary touch. I rubbed his hands, scaled from chemotherapy. I longed to go home and rub lotion on his hands. He had never been much of an emotional person, but that day was an exception. He caved in like a house on a sinkhole—just like me, he knew. All the wishes in the world wouldn't stop his stage four cancer from attacking every organ in his now frail body. Despite the pain, I was proud of him. He was not letting cancer win. He wanted to live. He refused to bring a wheelchair, turning the short trek from the entrance building to the gym into a marathon. He endured three hours driving—getting lost a couple times with screaming kids—to come here and find me.

We smiled in front of a beach-themed backdrop of an orange and yellow sunset on a horizon. There was a little sailboat riding against the waves and a big palm tree in the sand. There was a boardwalk along the beach. I wished I could take that boardwalk and go far away where cancer couldn't find us. I wished we were really in paradise. I wished there wasn't a Tsunami headed straight toward us.

I felt selfish because in those final moments—instead of being with my children like the other mothers—I lay on my dad's shoulder crying. I clung to him tightly just like when I was younger and wrapped myself around his leg while he walked around the house. Only this time he wasn't trying to shake me off. I sucked it up in the funnel of my mind like a tornado. The memories of us spun round and round in my mind. Tears of pain: The only thing being spit out. I was awed. He was my father, my hero, my best friend. The one man I never had to question depending on.

When my mom went to prison, my father stepped up. He took care of me. Picture it: A big, manly construction worker with calloused hands and a sad fragile little girl who just wanted her mom. He did it despite all the obstacles we faced, despite the fact he had no idea what he was doing. He didn't know how to comb my hair or what I liked to eat but we figured it out.

He would sit me at the table right next to him during his weekly poker games with the boys and teach me all about my poker face. I never had a good one but he did. He still had the best poker face on

Family Day. He wouldn't let me see his pain even though I imagine it was unbearable. He did his best.

I think the birthplace of all my creativity is his willingness to indulge me. He never told me I couldn't. He always believed in me and let me explore and figure things out for myself.

I wanted a clubhouse; he gave me wood and nails and let me create whatever my young mind could think up. It took me seven stitches from a hammer, but I had my clubhouse. Movie Director? My father bought me a video camera. It took me a hundred takes but I made my movie. Have you ever seen a Christmas tree decorated solely by an eight-year-old girl? You could say it's interesting. It was covered in lots of annoying icicles and fruity candy canes, decorated with whatever shiny bulbs he let me pick out at the Big Lots across town. On Christmas morning under the tree, there was exactly what I asked for. Nothing more, nothing less. He would stand watching me, rubbing his head with excitement when I became giddy, knowing he had pleased me.

He sang me his own little made up tunes every morning repeating, "It's time to get up for school." He taught me how to be a kid and I taught him how to be a parent.

My daughter, Adessa, never had her dad around, so she became my dad's, too. It was interesting because by then he knew all about raising a little girl. It gave me comfort to know she was overprotective of him at the Family Day visit, like I'm sure she was at home witnessing his decline. Adessa cared so much even in her adolescence that she trailed behind him going to the bathroom. When he dropped his oxygen tank she just picked it up casually like she did it all the time. She shouldn't have had to worry about oxygen tanks.

Despite my best efforts, I fell apart like New Orleans after Katrina. As I've said, I've never had a good poker face. I'm not as strong as my dad was.

Adessa rubbed my hair back in an attempt to comfort me as I wept. Onlookers invaded my moment with sympathetic smiles, then moved on because they knew there was nothing they could say. The oxygen tube curved across his body like a slithering serpent; it was a clear indicator that he was sick.

Yes, they went about the day. A day that was filled with joy for them. I was envious and it was pathetic. I was filled with nostalgic daydreams and what ifs. I wanted to know my dad would walk me down the aisle when I got married. However, as much as I wished it wasn't true, it would never happen. Cancer is a bitch.

When I leaned on his shoulder and smelled the faint linger of laundry soap I realized how heartless cancer is. How devastating, how hopeless. It was the stuff of nightmares and I still can't wake up. It was tearing through my family with an effortless force like ripping paper. Cancer didn't care that my dad was all I have ever had. All it cared about it was spreading, growing, slowly killing him. No treatment had been able to stop it and doubtful any treatment would. If he were a house after a flood, he would have been condemned. His insides would be covered in black mold. No matter how hard you scrubbed it, it would just keep coming back.

My dad died almost a year later. Cancer spread like a rumor from his lungs to his liver and eventually to his brain. I felt guilty for being in prison. I felt relieved he was at peace.

The day I wasn't expecting it, it happened. The day I didn't freak out when the phone just rang with no answer, it happened. Many times I had called and panicked when there was no answer, when really my dad had been racing around on a motorized wheelchair at the mall, his oxygen in the basket and his best friend, who also had cancer, right beside him. They were a pair, that's for sure. One day I called and my dad had just gotten back from a sports bar, drunk. He proceeded to tell me how at the bar he and Jerry smelled each other and proclaimed they didn't smell like death. Imagine what the bartender must have thought.

Just once I didn't freak out. I thought I knew better than to worry my ass off when really he was off somewhere being his ornery self. Maybe he was pushing his rickety walker to play the slots which he refused to admit triggered seizures. Maybe he was flirting with the nurses too much to answer the phone.

I went to a routine appointment in the worn down, grungy mental health building to renew my treatment plan. I couldn't imagine going through this without Prozac. Walking through the quiet corridor and up the stairs I never expected it. I was two minutes into the appointment when she got the call.

She was a newer counselor; I had barely brushed the surface of my problems with her. I was telling her about the slow torture that was my dad's cancer—the not knowing. The phone rang and I thought it was so rude to take a phone call during a session. Later she told me it was the most eerie feeling she's ever had. The odds that I would be sitting right there were slim to none. She said the words I had always known were coming. I tilted my head and just stared at her. This is it, my head said.

At first, I just looked at her confused. What did she just say? No tears boiled up. This is it, my head kept repeating as my heart began to race.

"I need you to call for Kansas Grube. She lives in Hale dorm."

The liaison didn't even question my request—just did it. Unusual treatment for an inmate.

"Are you okay?"

"I have been preparing for this for a long time," I told her.

Kansas hit the hallway outside the office. She had no idea who had called for her. I made eye contact with her. All I could say was: "He is gone."

"Oh, fuck," she responded. Kansas is a hardcore Christian; she never cusses. My mental health liaison—as far as I'm concerned—was not qualified to deal with me right then. Kansas was. She knew me, and she had heard enough stories that she knew him.

We walked to the chaplain's office together. You see the problem with God's timing is it's always perfect. I was scheduled for Kairos— the biggest Christian retreat on the prison farm—the next day. Kairos means "God's time." It was supposed to be a walk with God. Very few are selected to attend. There were 24 of us. I guess God wanted me to know for a fact that he was carrying me through this. I'd mourned since 2015. It had been slow agony every day, the uncertainty.

The thing about time is preparation: Nothing is left unsaid. I knew every time I talked to my dad it might be the last. I had the luxury of saying goodbye. I told that man how much I loved and adored him every day for two years.

"I know, Heather. You say it every five minutes," he would respond.

I got time to apologize and spill my soul to him for all the wrongs I had done during my rebellious years. I asked him what he wanted me to do with my life and he answered. I know what dreams he had for me. I know the life he wanted me to live.

I'm told he went peacefully in his sleep. I prayed for that relentlessly every day. I wanted God to end his suffering. People told me that in the end I would beg God to take him. I didn't believe them. Now I do. At the end, he was only exhaling every five minutes.

When I returned to the crowded dorm—surrounded, but alone—I told no one. Only Kansas knew. I didn't want pity. I almost craved it while he was sick. I wanted people to know I was suffering right along with him. I eventually told those close to me. All evening my friends comforted me, coming to my aid like the Red Cross. I surprised them with how calm I was. I surprised myself.

When I found out my dad had cancer, it was like a volcano of emotion erupted, threatening everything about my life. The lava slowly took over everything in its path, relentlessly. The cancer inched slowly, consuming my dad's body. Taunting my whole family with heat so close to our home. We could smell the plastic lawn chairs burning. We knew soon it would consume our lives and we would no longer be able to deny its lurking presence. We went over countless emergency drills in preparation. He always fought.

If I dared to picture what my life would be like after my father passed, I saw myself screaming and crying in distress, begging God to put the pieces of my internal city back together again. I never dared to imagine it was possible to rebuild a city after an eruption. When it happened, I found myself silently sweeping through the thick soot and picking up the wreckage. I was fully aware that the chaos was over and I could breathe. My pre-grief was hard. The death was expected.

Months later I am still learning to live without him. It still hits me like aftershock. I still dial his number on the phone only to realize he isn't going to answer. Grief sneaks up on me with something as simple as a treacherous commercial. "OPDIVO®," it says. "A chance to live longer." And then it thanks the patients of the clinical trials. OPDIVO® was the last thing my father tried. It didn't save him. He didn't find refuge. However—thanks to how he lived—I did. The memories of us keep me sane.

When I was about sixteen years old, I found myself soaked, walking aimlessly in the rain. I was in the middle of nowhere in Lubeck West Virginia with my friend Amanda, lugging a case of beer. My phone beeped, alerting me the battery was almost dead. I did what I always did: I called my dad. Drunk and frantic, I asked him to come get me. Problem was I didn't know where I was. I was coming down a back skirt black top road surrounded by woods to a clearing.

"Look around. What do you see?" my father asked.

I looked around and described to him what I saw. A little abandoned church with an overpass behind it up a steep hill. Then nothing, my phone had died. Amanda and I were both rebellious, both fighting a war with adolescent insecurities and fitting in. I don't know why we left the party, maybe somebody pissed us off or maybe we just got bored of the usual beer pong and drunk advances. I do know Amanda and I had found ourselves lost, sitting on a curb drinking cheap beer while the wind and rain fought around us. We were out of options. We couldn't find our way back and we couldn't find our way to the main road. We were stuck in a drunken maze. The highway taunted us from up the hill with sounds of passing cars. The hill was an impossible trek.

For a moment we had forgotten where we were. We just enjoyed the rain and the beer. We were living young and careless. Amanda yelled into the empty church parking lot.

"Helloooooo out there!"

"Aughhhhh," I yelled, impersonating George of the Jungle.

God himself was probably laughing at us in that deserted church parking lot.

Eventually, a horn's blare answered us from the highway above. We looked up the steep hill to see my dad's little blue Dodge Dakota two-seated truck with it's rusted steel toolbox pulled over on the shoulder of the highway. The window was rolled down and he was honking down at us. He was yelling, prompting us to climb up the hill. Amanda and I just looked at each other, then at the soggy case of beer. Fuck it.

Amanda's drunk ass had the idea to put the beer up her soaked hoodie. We thought we were so slick and so inconspicuous. Amanda and I began to trek up the hill to the truck, falling and sliding down the wet grass. She was struggling with the beer. One falling out here and there. We were trying to grip onto flimsy grass only for it to rip from the ground. My dad was rooting us on the whole time like we were on the three-yard line at the Superbowl. Finally, we reached the top, feeling triumphant. We were soaked with rain and sweat. We stumbled over the barrier and flung the case of beer into the back of the truck as if my dad didn't hear the thump, and as if he didn't see it fall out of Amanda's hoodie and roll down the rill right along with us during our failed attempts to scale the hill. But we eventually made it. We got in the cab acting casual like my dad hadn't just rescued drunk us from the middle of nowhere.

She was on the seat. I sat on the console of the small truck close enough to my dad that my wet clothes were seeping into his.

"You girls didn't bring a case of beer with you did you?" he asked, smiling. He wasn't stupid but he played dumb. Now that he had found us he was done with the worry. He had moved onto entertainment.

"No, Daddy."

I managed to get the radio on and we drunkenly sang all the way to town. "To the window, to the wall," we sang in our Lil Jon voices.

When we came onto abandoned seventh street it was late, deserted. My dad took us through Hardee's fast food restaurant. He was cool like that. It was open 24 hours. We ordered their famous six dollar burger with greasy curly fries and large, thick, strawberry milkshakes with whip cream and lots of apple turnovers. My dad just laughed and paid.

We stumbled into the house. My dad ushered us to the kitchen table where we ate our food like homeless people at a soup kitchen. Then he made us go to bed, which really consisted of us drunkenly laying in my queen size bed talking about what-ifs, watching the ceiling spin. "Y'all alright?" he kept yelling up the stairs every time the floor creaked from movement.

We answered "yeah" down the attic stairs, half annoyed. He just cackled.

I knew he was rubbing his head, his signature gesture. Happy, sad, mad: He always rubbed his head frantically. A quirk I truly cherish now.

My dad always found me. ALWAYS. So even in death, even when I die, I know he will find me. I know when I'm lonely and missing him he will find me. Even if it's only in my dreams, he will always find me.

The most exciting part of receiving the Writing for Justice Fellowship from PEN America was being the possibility of being a part of—and less apart from—the literary community. I sincerely hope, as time goes on, I can further feel not only that I belong, but that I am making meaningful contributions of work to that community and tradition, beyond being recognized and appreciated mostly—or solely—for my contributions as a "prison writer." I think, if you want to change the narrative surrounding writers in prison, programs and organizational mechanisms and practices need to continue to push us to write beyond prison. By that I don't mean the content shouldn't be centered in the institutions that have shaped our lives so tangibly, but that the bar should be set high enough to demand quality work over the possible tokenized inclusion of marginalized voices, and the resources made available to us should reflect that demand. The literary community as a whole should continue to ask tough questions about its role in responsibly cultivating and giving audience to the voices of incarcerated writers. Some of these questions might be: How can we make it easier to find and submit to our platforms? What can we do to match up the work of incarcerated writers to publications that will appreciate the individual works? And what steps can we take to push incarcerated writers beyond the "prison writer" label and into the mainstream literary fray, while still honoring the stories and content that come from the prison experience?

— Jusin Rovillos Monson,
2017 Honorable Mention in Poetry,
PEN America Prison Writing Awards and
2018 PEN America Writing For Justice Fellow

2019 PEN AMERICA PRISON WRITING AWARDS IN NONFICTION **ESSAY**

First Prize, Essay

Thorazine, Haldol & Coffee: My Life in a Prison Mental Health Ward

MICHAEL KAISER

The idea that I would ever be working in the mental ward of a state prison or any mental ward—or for that matter, be in prison—was totally foreign to me. I was a somewhat successful real estate developer who had also worked for two U.S. Presidents.

But then I found myself in prison for 60 months, and I needed a job. The only requirement for the Intermediate Care Housing (ICH) Daily Living Orderly job was that I had no sex offences in my background. I didn't, so I was hired.

I had seen One flew over the Cuckoos Nest. Hell, a fellow Oregonian had written it, and I could look out my window and see what was left of the original state hospital where the movie was filmed. Now I would be tending to men who would have been housed in that institution, but instead they were in prison. My six days of training consisted of learning how to properly lift a man who had fallen and helping to change adult diapers. That was it. As far as the prison was concerned I was ready for work. I had been given more training for the volunteer work I did at a local food bank prior to prison.

ICH is designed as a stepping-stone for inmates with mental health issues prior to either going home or into the general prison population. When the security officer opened the door, and I walked into the unit, I had no idea what I'd find and what to do.

That first day, I half expected to meet at least one Danny Devito or Jack Nicholson type from Cuckoos Nest. (That would come later). I imagined there would be a Nurse Ratched on the ward. In fact, there was no nurse at all. In this unit where every resident was deemed unfit for general population because their mental illness made them a risk, either to themselves or others, there was no medical or mental health staff in sight.

For the most part, the unit setup was no different than for the general prison population: one wall lined with thirty-eight 6 x 8 foot cells, each with a single bed, a television enclosed in a metal box (I would find out why later) a toilet, and a sink. The doors were barred not solid. What was different was that right outside the cells were seven tables, hot water for coffee and games. The guys had the luxury of being out of their cells twice a day for two hours of dayroom.

After the officer let me in, he went back to watching whatever it was on YouTube that was engrossing him and the other officers. He nodded to the cells like I knew what to do next. I didn't. But I had to do something. So I went cell to cell introducing myself to each of the 38 residents. There were guys as young as 18 and as old as 75. In the first two cells, the guys were asleep. In cell three I met Barry: balding, big head, big belly and a great laugh. Think of Homer Simpson. Standing in front of his cell I see at least 10 variations of the same painting taped to his wall: black background, white star in the middle and a red lighting bolt in the middle the star, each painting a little work of art.

No more than two minutes into our conversation I was hearing about the encounter between heaven's angels and the demons of hell that Barry had witnessed in August of 2005. Each picture represented what he had seen that night. It was important for him to make sure that I knew all this was real and that he was not a freak.

A few cells later, I was met with the greeting, "Hey Chucky." My first thought was that someone had told these guys my name was Chucky. Then a second later, I heard "where's the cheese?" Sitting on the bunk was 350 plus pounds of kid-man with a face that seemed to have never had a worry in the world. Not a wrinkle. Even when he laughed that huge laugh, there were no laugh lines in the corner of his eyes. I couldn't tell if he was 25 or 55. Later I would find out that he called everyone Chucky, that his name was Kenny, that he was 51 and had been in prison for 31 years, that he had escaped once (or not) and would stop anyone at anytime to tell them a joke (almost always inappropriate).

I made a point that first day to speak to everyone who was awake. That was a promise I made to myself that day, and I've carried it through for the past two years.

Thirty-eight cells and an hour later was Howie. The unofficial mayor of the penitentiary, he seemed to know everyone and had never met a microphone that he didn't like. Whether it is Mass or an Alcoholics Anonymous meeting, Howie had something to say. And that "something" would invariably include that he had spent 23 years in prison, that "some big people had put me in prison and some big people will get me out," and that he had half a brain and half a heart and could die any minute. I have stopped myself more than once from reminding him if he really had only half a heart and half a brain he would be dead.

Howie had spent a lifetime in and out of minor trouble, all connected to mental disease. Added to his schizophrenia was paranoia and added to that were homicidal thoughts. In early October 1995 his probation officer asked the court to remand Howie to a psychiatrist who, after meeting with him, was concerned enough that he asked a judge to order a six-month stay in a psychiatric hospital. Twelve days into his stay and seven days before Christmas, after the state had refused to continue paying for the private hospital where he was housed, he was released. Three days later he killed the first person he felt had disrespected him. Then he sat on the sidewalk and waited for the police to arrive. His first words to the officer were, "I told them not to let me go."

I don't remember the day I met Roger. He was transferred into the unit from MHI (Mental Health Infirmary) months after I began working. A thin man in his fifties with glasses so thick that his eyes looked the size of quarters, Roger could be the nicest guy in the world or the worst. His mood revolved around a cup of tea. If he had one, all things were good. If not: watch out, I have seen him attack the first person he sees. I have seen him break a television into countless pieces (he's the reason the televisions are housed in steel boxes with protective glass covers). He was one of the few people in the unit the courts had originally sent to the state mental hospital. He spent six years there before the state, in a cost cutting measure ($150,000 per year vs. $40,000) decided that he was okay for prison. He fought the move and actually won a court case, but he remained in prison. His original 70-month robbery sentence has turned into a 16-year stretch because of minor—and some not so minor—infractions, almost all connected to his mental instability. Now he has spent so much time in solitary that the openness of the ICH unit scares him. He is afraid to be around people. When it becomes too much he goes to extremes to return to the Mental Health Infirmary. He has assaulted fellow inmates, swallowed six radio batteries (interesting X-Ray) and even ate a radio, which resulted in a hospital run and surgery. Even though it's not part of my job, I have the tea ready for when he returns.

One thing I learned quickly was that everyone on the unit is not seeing things, hearing things or sitting on their beds rocking back and forth. Some act as "normal" as anyone, usually thanks to massive doses of antipsychotics. These are usually the saddest stories and often the most dangerous guys. Miguel is one of these people. He was about to finish his undergraduate degree in Japanese Studies, had a job, his own house and a family who loved him. That all changed on a September morning ten years ago when he was 22. While working the graveyard shift at a local market, the shirt of a customer became a hologram. From there, things progressed to him believing that he was a god who had special powers to make his college team win or lose games. I asked him if he thought all this odd. One second you're selling a guy a pack of cigarettes and the next you're a god. He told me that in his mind all this was normal and to him it was just the way things were. For two years the disease progressed to the point where he saw conspiracy and insults in everything said to him. Eight days before Christmas, he knew someone had to die. The next day he murdered his roommate as she was sitting at her laptop writing an email to her daughter.

Schizophrenia doesn't discriminate.

Some are born with it; many others like Miguel experience symptoms in their early adulthood. I worried about him the first day we met. I still do. His medication has stopped the symptoms, but it has allowed him to look at and relive every action he has taken as a spectator. One night months after we first met he looked at me and asked, "Am I going to Hell?" How do I answer that? One thing I knew for sure: Theological questions were not part of my weeklong training. I don't lie to these guys, so I answered as honestly as I knew how, "I don't know, but I hope not." I wish that I could say that I had told him that God forgives everything, and all you have to do is ask. I didn't. If God made these guys minds, he has to take some responsibility for them. Miguel has the possibility of leaving here after serving a twenty-five year sentence. He will be forty-nine. But he's a "Dreamer", not a citizen, and Immigration has put a deportation hold on him. He came to America at age five. His three sisters are United States citizens. If he is deported, he will be alone with a mental disease in a country he doesn't know.

And then there is Gene. He is never going to be mistaken for just one of the guys, not even by ICH standards. Unless it's for medication or a meal, he never leaves his cell.

There are days when Gene does nothing but sit on his bed and stare at his cell wall. It took me more than a year of talking to him everyday on my rounds just to get him to acknowledge that I existed. To Gene, some days I am Michael, some days I am Matt. Michael is the guy who, after a year, Gene handed a bottle of strawberry jam as a gift, told him that he was the only friend that he had ever had in prison and that he loved him.

Matt is someone from his past who was an important part of his life. One day he will ask Michael to help him write a letter to Matt. The next day he will give me that letter telling me "Hey Matt I have a letter for you." I wonder why and how Gene ended up in prison, and what his old life was like. I know for a fact that the Gene I know is not capable of taking care of himself, When and if he speaks, he is incoherent. His conversation can go from monster trucks to butterflies in a matter of seconds and make total sense to Gene.

Did mental disease hit him in his twenties like it did Miguel? There are times he will tell me about things that he has done, jobs he's had in such detail that I know he can't be making it up. I also know that there is no way the Gene I know is capable of doing any of these things. Who could have thought that prison was a better place for Gene than the state mental hospital?

The first time I met Michael, another man in the unit, I showed him a picture of Grant Woods painting American Gothic. I thought he looked like the skinny guy with the pitchfork. Michael told me he was better looking and would never wear overalls.

Michael came into the unit not long after arriving in prison. He was one of those guys who the corrections department didn't know where to house. He had mental issues, so mainline wasn't an option, but he was also highly functional. He had a relatively short sentence of seventy months with twenty percent deducted for good time and just wanted to get back home to his dog. Michael was a pain in the ass. He was all about his schedule. I had put a list on his cell wall giving times for everything from meals to evening medication line. To Michael when I had put 6:00 as the time for evening dayroom it meant 6:00 PM not 6:01. If things happened even a minute late he would start yelling that he had been forgotten. Trying to explain why the door hadn't opened was an exercise in futility, 6:00 PM was 6:00 PM, period.

In the unit when one guy gets sick they all get sick. A cold can start at one end of the unit, go from cell to cell, get to the end and start all over again Even though each man has his own cell, the guys are together many hours each day for meals, dayroom and showers.

You can't live in such close proximity to 38 other people and not catch something. Late January was one of those times. Michael didn't look good. He complained of vertigo and that something was "wrong" with his breathing. It was not part of my job description, but I made a medical appointment for Michael the last Friday of January. When you are in prison and sick, you seldom see a doctor. You see a nurse, or if you're lucky a nurse practitioner. Michael thought he got lucky. His appointment was with a nurse practitioner who was pretty new and hopefully was not yet jaded. He didn't think he could walk from the unit to medical so I grabbed a wheelchair and we headed to the appointment. The appointment was at 2:45 but she was running late, which became a big issue for Michael. When he finally got in, his first words to the nurse practitioner were "help me, I can't breathe, I need to stay in the infirmary." She listened to his chest. His vitals were not great but nothing to worry about, she told him. She knew that Michael had come from the mental health unit. Maybe she thought that Michael was overreacting. She told him she would prescribe an antibiotic, that he should drink plenty of water, and he could go back to the unit. That was the first time I saw Michael cry, begging to be allowed to stay, sobbing as I wheeled him across the control room floor back to the unit.

Wednesday he wasn't any better. I had made sure he was drinking water and would help him sit up on his bed, but something was still wrong. I asked the officer to call medical and see if I could bring him up. Same story, different day: Michael crying asking to stay in the infirmary. This time a nurse telling him that he was "too sick" and she didn't want him in "her" infirmary getting other people sick. He was told to continue drinking water and go back to his cell. On Sunday afternoon, when I checked on him, Michael looked awful. His skin was gray, and his breathing labored. When I woke him, he said he had not eaten or drank anything since I had left the day before and that no one had checked on him. I noticed a dinner tray from the night before had been pushed under his door and was sitting on the floor untouched. I sat him up on his bed, got him a glass of water and made sure that he drank as much as he could. He knew who I was, but something was different, I could tell he was afraid, but he didn't cry or ask to go to the infirmary. For the next four hours, I did what I always did, walk up and down the tier talking to the guys who want to talk, getting cups of hot water for the guys who wanted it and also checking on Michael to make sure he sat up and had water.

Three times a day a nurse who that day has been assigned to the ICH unit, wheeled a cart full of pills into the unit and distributed whatever medication the psychiatrist or medical doctors had prescribed the guys. I call it med line; the guys call it "Happy Hour." She arrived at 7:00 PM, the same time I needed to leave the unit and shower. (In prison showering is like peeing, you do it when you can, not when you have to.) I asked the unit officer to make sure that the nurse knew that Michael was unable to walk to the medication cage to get his meds and that I would be back as soon as I could. You would think that the security staff would have special training to work in a mental health unit. They don't. In fact, some security officers bid on the job thinking they'll have an "easy" shift where they can hide out for eight hours and play dominos with the guys. But there are also some officers who really care about how inmates in special housing are treated and try their best. When I returned to the unit from the shower, I saw the nurse at Michael's cell and Ms. Steele, a security officer who was only in the unit for that Sunday night, sitting on Michael's bed, rubbing his hands and telling the nurse that "this man has to see a doctor." Michael's hands and arms had swollen to almost double in size in the twenty minutes I had been gone. He was still aware but becoming less so.

"He will be okay. Just make sure he has liquids," I heard the nurse say.

"No, he needs a doctor," Ms. Steele said. "If I need to contact the Officer in Charge, I will. Look at his arms!" Ms. Steele wasn't a nurse, but she knew sick when she saw it.

The nurse didn't budge. "He has an appointment tomorrow morning, and he will be fine til then." she said. When the nurse left, Ms. Steele made that call to the officer in charge of the prison. I don't know what she said to him. It was after 8:30 PM and work was over. I had been in the unit on and off for almost 11 hours by then and had to be back early the next morning to take Michael to his medical appointment.

Five hours before I was to officially start my shift, I was back in the unit with a wheelchair ready to take Michael to his appointment. His skin was gray, his limbs were puffy. I asked the officer to open his cell so that I could wake him. He knew who I was.

He wouldn't take a drink of water. I helped him into the wheelchair for the three-minute trip to medical and what I hoped would soon be a trip downtown to the city hospital.

When we were less than ten feet away from the cell, his head slumped to the right, he started gasping for air, and piss started running from the seat of the chair to the floor. I yelled for the Sergeant, who called "man down" (the prison equivalent to stat in a hospital), Medical was called. Twelve minutes later they arrived. Michael was put on a stretcher and wheeled out of the unit. That was the last time I saw him. He finally got that hospital trip he had been asking for. He died there the next morning.

Michael's death hit me hard, not because we were great friends, but because it was unnecessary. Three different medical staff ignored or downplayed the pleas of a very sick man for the help he surely would have received except for being in prison and—even worse—being in prison with a mental disease. Could I have done anything differently? Did Ms. Steele do all she could? Will his family ever know the story of what happened? How many Michaels have there been in this institution? At other prisons around the country?

It's been more two years since I walked onto the ICH unit. Half the guys who were there then still are. A few others have done well enough to go to general population.

Some of the others have been lucky enough to go home. More than I'd like to think about have gotten worse. I've stopped asking questions of the staff. They ignored them, told me to mind my own business, or sometimes gave me truthful answers that wish I hadn't heard. Why did Barry spend three years of his life in prison only to have all his charges dropped three weeks after his release? Why is Gene spending five years in prison for a crime he has no recollection of? Now that his sentence is coming to an end, the state has decided to commit him, involuntarily, to the state mental hospital. Why does the system work this way?

A few decades ago there were 325,000 people in mental hospitals in the United States. Today that number is less than 50,000. Have 275,000 been cured? Or are tens of thousands of them in prison? Those with mental illnesses who might come to prison for a short sentence sometimes end up staying for decades. They don't get consistent counseling. They don't get consistent medication. They act out. In the depths of schizophrenia, seeing monsters, cowering in the corner of his cell, a man spits on an officer. Punishment for an assault against a staff is added to the end of his current sentence, each infraction adding more time. Why is it that officers can work in a mental health unit with no extra training? Why is it that if one of the guys has a mental meltdown after 8:00 PM or anytime on Sunday there is no mental health staff at the institution?

Why was Michael allowed to die?

I can't tell you the day that my work in ICH changed from being just a job. Michael's death had something to do with it, but it wasn't only that. These men on the unit are friends. I look forward to seeing them each day. Maybe in some small way, I am making a difference. But it also may be that I get more out of being with them than they do by having me there. This job is helping me survive prison.

Second Prize, Essay

Death By Incarceration: Cruel and Unusual

RICHARD GROSS

Death By Incarceration is the name we give the sentence of Life Without the Possibility of Parole (LWOP). We call it that because it is a death sentence—as sure to end in death as any method of execution. It is the other death penalty, the slow death penalty, or the "hidden death penalty" as Pope Francis called it when he condemned LWOP.

Considered by many to be a humane alternative to execution, in reality, it is no different. Many people on death row sit there for decades with a death sentence hanging over them but ultimately die of natural causes. Regardless of the cause of death, if someone enters a prison never to leave there alive, it is a death sentence. Prison sentences that exceed the normal length of a human life should also be considered a death penalty. Many more people have been sentenced to death than anyone realizes.

Pennsylvania has 10% of this nation's lifers, over 5,000 men and women sentenced to Death by Incarceration in a state with less than 5% of the nation's population. The average lifetime incarceration costs the Commonwealth $3.6 million. Multiply that by the number of lifers and Pennsylvania's taxpayers are on the hook for 19 billion dollars. See Temple University Professor Emeritus Kay Harris' research on the economics of life sentences.

What I can speak to is the human toll. The men who have slowly lost their minds locked in a 7 x 12 cage for several decades. The children and grandchildren of lifers who grow to adulthood without having their parent or grandparent at any birthday party, graduation, or wedding. No one does a life sentence by themselves. Their friends and loved ones serve time as well.

I think we need to ask ourselves a few pertinent questions. What are prisons for? Are prisons a place of endless punishment, or are they a place where those who pose a risk to others are separated from society until they no longer pose a threat? Is prison a place where people are corrected and rehabilitated? If so, then what part do death sentences play in that? If there is no chance of parole than those sentences are not about corrections or rehabilitation, but are only about retribution and revenge.

Thousands of Pennsylvania's lifers are beyond the point where they would, or in many cases even could, pose a threat to society. Older people who have served some significant time have an extremely low rate of recidivism—a negligible rate. There is a point where society no longer needs protection from the person. After that point, the taxpayers are not being well-served by the cost of the incarceration. These costs often skyrocket as the person grows old in prison and their health deteriorates. With family and friends unable to assist, the burden of their care falls to the state. It is unconstitutional to deny an incarcerated person healthcare. One has to assume that the individual would be able to access and afford proper health care were they not incarcerated.

It is true, however, that many free, taxpaying citizens cannot afford health insurance.

So, wouldn't health care be a better use of taxpayer dollars than incarceration? The Pennsylvania Department of Corrections' budget is $2.4 billion. Double what is was a decade ago. Unless parole is used more often or sentencing changes are made, it will only grow larger. Mass incarceration has drained taxpayer dollars away from healthcare, education, and infrastructure in order to build more prisons. These prisons become major providers of both mental health and geriatric care. Pennsylvania has over 6,000 geriatric prisoners and that number will only grow as long as death by incarceration is used so regularly.

In cases of first or second degree murder, a jury has no choice but to hand down a death sentence. The parole board has no choice when it comes to releasing a life-sentenced prisoner—regardless of age, infirmity, transformation, or time served. In our nation's zeal to be tough on crime, we have taken away the discretion once practiced by prosecutors, judges, juries, and parole boards. "Lock 'em up and throw away the key" sounds good to many voters as a campaign slogan, but as policy, it is neither humane nor cost effective. In a rational cost/ benefit analysis, it makes no sense to send fifteen-year-olds to prison for the rest of their natural life, nor does it make sense to keep senior citizens locked up until they die.

Other states in this region have significantly lowered their prison populations without experiencing an increase in their crime rate. Applying risk assessment methods, parole boards can safely release both violent and non-violent offenders. They just have to be allowed and encouraged to do so by the elected officials of their state. A parole board has nothing to gain by releasing a dangerous person and can be trusted with the power to evaluate every incarcerated person. In Pennsylvania, between 1967 and 2017 hundreds of lifers received commutation and were granted parole. Only one came back with a felony. Numerous juvenile lifers have recently been released successfully after being granted relief by the courts. These men and women are not the same people they were as teenagers, and they are already making a positive contribution to their communities. America's fear of people on parole is unfounded and irrational.

Most incarcerated persons have experienced dramatic transformations during their incarceration. This is especially true of lifers. Among them you can find great artists and writers. Scholars and academics. Facilitators and creators of positive programs which make a difference in the lives of people who do get released. There are lifers who have created murals and charitable organizations on the outside, from the inside. The achievements of lifers are extensive and worthy of recognition. The Philadelphia City Council has commended the lifers organization at SCI Graterford. Numerous individual lifers have won awards for creative writing and artwork produced behind bars. Dozens have earned degrees from Villanova University and elsewhere. Many others have completed ministry and Bible study courses from a variety of religious organizations. Lifers create and lead non-profit groups that do positive work both inside and outside of prison, like Let's Circle Up. The general public knows little about these because the wall around the jail keeps them out as much as it keeps others in.

Anyone can recognize these good deeds and personal transformations—except a parole board. They are prohibited from examining the achievements and the rehabilitation of any individual serving a death by incarceration sentence. No matter how much good they may hear, they cannot recognize or reward it. Even if there is support for release from the victim's family, local clergy, and the community at large, they can do nothing. Their hands are tied by retributive sentencing policies.

It seems to me that any person drawing a breath on planet earth must be seen by the supreme being as having some good in them, some possibility of redemption. I know that all human beings are capable of change. Are our leaders, legislators, and prosecutors the same people now that they were decades ago? I know that no person is the same person that they were 15 or 20 years ago. Is it humane, is it right, is it even rational to judge an entire human life by the worst ten minutes of it?

In the Pennsylvania State legislature, House Bill 135 and Senate Bill 942 seek to recognize the power of human beings to transform themselves. Representative Dawkins and Senator Street have introduced these companion bills which would allow all lifers to be considered for parole on a case by case basis. This is no "get out of jail free" card. This is merely a chance for lifers to show the parole board what they have done with themselves during their incarceration. Just a chance to be seen, to be heard, to be noticed as still alive and human.

Any type of death sentence is cruel. For the state to take a human life or to lock someone up until they are dead is cruel. It is a rejection of reform, rehabilitation, and redemption. It is the act of throwing away a human being, discarding a person. It is a denial of humanity. Any type of death sentence is unusual.

Most nations have no kind of death sentence. Nowhere in the European Union is this occurring. The longest possible sentence in Norway is 21 years. In Germany a murderer can expect parole after fifteen years if they have followed their personalized rehabilitation plan. Nowhere in the Americas is this occurring except in the United States. Few places in the world outside of the United States have life without parole. No nation that I know of would give it to a juvenile. These types of death sentences are rare, unusual, and becoming more so as civilization advances. These death sentences have no place in any humane society.

To place a human being in prison until death is in fact cruel and unusual punishment.

146

Third Prize, Essay

Mass Incarceration: The Shame of a Nation
SANTONIO MURFF

United States District Judge William Schwarzer has never been known as a light sentencer. So to see his usually stoic demeanor crumble into choked tears on the bench shocked a San Francisco courtroom to silence...

Judge Lawrence Irving, a career crime fighter, had been face-to-face with criminals and the consequences of their actions for decades when he abruptly retired, stating: "If I remain on the bench, I have no choice but to follow the law. I just can't, in good conscience, continue to do this."

Judge Jack Weinstein also publicly refused to participate further, describing "a sense of depression about much of the cruelty" that he'd been party to from his exalted position on the bench.

Judge Stanley Marshall, always considered a fairly harsh sentencer, echoed similar sentiments to a reporter, admitting: "It's killing me..."

What could reduce a sitting judge to tears or force another into retirement? Leave one depressed while slowly spiritually killing another?

Mass Incarceration, the shame of our nation, is the callous and calculating culprit guilty on all fronts. The much bemoaned mandatory minimums, three strikes, and habitual laws have worked hand in-hand with overzealous, ambitious, and sometimes unscrupulous prosecutors to explode our prison population over thirty years, from around 300,000 inmates in 1982 to a ridiculously embarrassing 2,300,000 in 2012.

Supreme Court Justice Anthony Kennedy best summed up the distraught judges' misgivings at a 2003 American Bar Association's annual gathering, when he stated:

"I can accept neither the necessity nor the wisdom of Federal mandatory minimum sentences. In all too many cases mandatory minimums are unjust!"

Testimonies and protests from sitting, retired, and Supreme Justices across our mighty nation—those Honorable souls of wisdom and integrity who we've entrusted to relegate justice—have agreed with Supreme Court Justice Kennedy's further condemnation of a foul and failed system "whose resources are misspent, punishments too severe, and sentences too loaded."

So why, then, are these draconian sentencing practices and laws of injustice still on the books? Why were they enacted to begin with? Most importantly, how are we going to repeal them, clear up this embarrassing blemish upon our national souls, and abolish this great shame that has left us guilty of putting more of our countrymen, women, and children in chains than any other civilized nation in the history of the world?

As I attempt to stimulate an open and honest dialogue (in hopes of creating a movement that will encourage change through sensible sentencing practices, and a more conscientious focus on care rather than cages, rehabilitation instead of revenue), I will answer those questions and more. We will delve deep beneath cold facts and figures usually exercised by academics, in order to unearth the real motivations of the people succeeding behind those numbers. We will also meet some of the real people suffering behind those numbers, too.

We will explore the driving force behind the prison industrial complex and the why of it all. We will examine the necessary steps we must unite around and execute as a nation to fell this eighty billion dollar behemoth that feeds upon the stolen potential and dashed dreams of U.S. citizens. This sinful corruptor that has sunk us so low that we are now investing in the failure of our young and forsaking our righteous creed of freedom and justice for finances and jobs.

The forefathers would be appalled, as should we all.

Four score and seven years ago our forefathers set forth on this continent a new nation conceived in liberty. It is time for us to return to those founding principles, and distribute them equally to all. It is time for us, as patriots, to put aside all fears, differences, and grievances, and do what is best for our country. To first understand how and why we—the world's lone super power—ended up with a prison population that dwarfs every other civilized country on the planet, we must look back to another dark, challenging period in our young nation's history.

As we triumphed then over the twin tyrants of hypocrisy and bigotry, so too, shall we find our way to taste victory against the malevolent machinations that have divided and maligned us with mass incarceration, the shame of a nation.

The year was 1865...

It was a long and bloody struggle, full of heroes and heroines of different hues and heroics. They risked it all, some even making the ultimate sacrifice to dine on the sweet fruit of freedom and hear the laughter of liberty on the lips of all from sea to shining sea. And then, with the mighty stroke of a presidential pen, the 13th Amendment to the U.S. Constitution freed some four million slaves.

In the blink of an eye, a nation within a nation was created. Having been forbidden by law to learn how to read and write under penalty of death, over 90% of the freshly liberated slaves were illiterate. Having never known the liberties and responsibilities of freedom, they were mostly at a loss for what to do with themselves. And the country was at a loss for what to do with them.

The U.S. Constitution and the Bill of Rights were written by caucasian men aged twenty-one years or older for caucasian men aged twenty-one or older. The United States of America was founded by caucasian men who intended for caucasian men to forever govern and rule their new nation. Honest Abe Lincoln best defined the mindstate of the times when he stated: "Someone must rule. And I, like any man, am for the White man being the ruler."

So, following the civil war, the question of the day was, 'What institutions, laws, or customs would be necessary to maintain control now that slavery was gone?"

Legal scholar Reva Siegal dubbed it "preservation through transformation." A process through which white privilege (and rule) is maintained through rules (laws) and rhetoric change. Black Codes, Grandfather Clauses, poll taxes, vagrancy laws, convict leasing, Jim Crow—these were are all forms of social controls created by politicians, implemented by the courts, and bolstered and enforced by the law (police officers) for the first century after emancipation, in order to keep the newly freed slaves disenfranchised, marginalized, and enslaved into a state of second-class citizenship at best; and a new, modernized for world eyes form of slavery at worst.

The struggle continued...

The year was 1965...

Only one hundred years later, educated and elevated with everything but a true knowledge of self, nationality, and sovereignty, the new Black nation of ex-slaves had caught its stride. At a loss no longer, Black progress and pride was on the rise. All across the land, they were refusing to be denied the inalienable rights to life, liberty, and the pursuit of happiness. They were demanding equality and a say-so at the polls.

The sleeping giant had awakened and was proving that they were willing to die so their children could enjoy all the liberties, rights, equalities, and privileges that every other American citizen enjoyed. By the hundreds, the thousands, and the millions they came. Different characters, differents faiths, different schools of thought—but they all came demanding one thing: Change!

The Black Muslims of The Nation of Islam were manifesting highly educated, faithful and fearless entrepreneurs who were boldly calling the wilderness of North America out for her devilish treatment of the so-called negroes...

The Black Panther Party for Self Defense—the vanguard of the Black militant groups like The Revolutionary Action Movement, African Liberation Day Movement, and The United Slaves (U.S.)—were marching with assault rifles, shotguns, and a firm understanding of the U.S. Constitution and State Penal Codes, demanding equal justice under the law. J. Edgar Hoover, then head of the F.B.I., called them the greatest threat to national security.

A Black King came with a righteous dream. His fiery, poetic prose moved millions forward with him—Black, White, and Other—to prick the conscience of a nation still struggling to find its way. Their non-violent protests and prayers were met with such savage barbarics that the true patriots, true souls of righteousness came together, once again, to inspire the mighty stroke of that presidential pen, and do what was right, and live up to the high principles espoused by the forefathers in two of the greatest documents ever written: The U.S. Constitution and The Bill of Rights.

Again, it had been a long, bloody struggle full of heroes and heroines of different hues and heroics, but change did come in the form of granted privileges as The Civil Rights Bill of 1964 was signed into law. Jim Crow, like slavery before it, had been dealt a death blow. The question of yesterday was again revisited with a vengeance: what new institutions, rules, and customs would be necessary to maintain control now that Jim Crow was gone?

Are the patterns becoming clear now? And the why of it all?

Allow me to make it even clearer. Prisons became the new institutions. Mandatory minimums, three strikes, and habitual laws became the new rules. Bigotry and hypocrisy remained the customs. "Criminal" became the new racially-coded rhetoric. And, yes, mass incarceration became the new tool...

And now that we know the why of it all, let's get to the whos!

J. Edgar Hoover launched COINTELPRO, a top secret Counterintelligence Program, which was ultra-successful, through nefarious and illegal means, in its objective of neutralizing government dissidents and organizations opposed to the status quo of white supremacy. Malcolm X, the face and voice of the Black Muslims, was assassinated. Martin Luther King, the face and voice of the Christians and The Civil Rights movement, was assassinated. The Black Panthers and other militants were infiltrated and decimated.

The civil unrest and rebellions of the 1960's and 70's were over. The majority of Black Leaders, the nurturers and guiders of the youth, were dead or in prison. The majority of the remainders settled down with their pacifiers of civil rights and integration and went back to sleep. The ever vigilant and conspiring ruling elite got busy with their plans for forming a new system of social control.

"You have to face the fact that the whole problem is really the Blacks. The key is to devise a system that recognizes this while not appearing to," now-disgraced President Richard Nixon emphasized to H.R. Haldeman, one of his key advisors.

The merits and morality of the Black's struggle, and the reasonableness of their demands, were irrelevant to the Commander-in-chief, as it had always been to the vast majority of those who sat in that seat before him. Especially in the southern states, blind eyes were turned to the inequalities and injustices that came as a birthright to Black Americans. A century later the "someone must rule" mentality was still prevalent among caucasian males, and there could not be white rule without Black control.

This is the demented school of thought that we must do away with in order to dismantle mass incarceration and peacefully coexist as a prosperous nation. The great fears of amalgamation of the races, the great pains perpetuated by slavery and Jim Crow, the great hatred harbored after the civil war—we must come together to communicate and heal and ensure that our young nation will no longer have to transverse these dark roads.

I know race relations is an uncomfortable subject matter for most, and is highly emotional for others, but we had to take that short sojourn so that you can understand that our criminal justice system is not in need of mere reforms, because it's not broken. This new criminal injustice system is doing exactly what it was designed to do; exactly what Jim Crow and slavery did before it. Mass incarceration, the new tool of control, is permanently locking a huge percentage of Blacks out of mainstream society; not only physically for a time, but also economically and political, even after they are released from the new institutions and prisons.

And, yes, having been moved from the auction blocks to the stock markets, huge profits are still being made for the few at the expense of the multitudes.

As Michelle Alexander explains in The New Jim Crow, "The emergence of each new system of control may seem sudden, but history shows that the seeds are planted long before each new institution begins to grow." Richard Nixon only planted the seeds, testing the soils of bigotry for President Ronald Reagan to declare our current war on drugs, which many credibly argue is no more than a war on Blacks, with a nominal amount of room for poor whites to also be sucked up by the complex prison industry.

The success of a multitude of Blacks in this same period in no way negates the argument, because, as sociologist Loic Wacquet puts it, "With each reincarnation of the controlling system, it is less total, less capable of encompassing and controlling an entire race.

Yes, the 13th Amendment did abolish slavery, but it left an often ignored loophole: slavery to this very day is perfectly legal and appropriate for those convicted of a crime. It is that exception which was seized upon by the evil minds who redesigned what was touted as the best legal system in the world, rendering it the most embarrassing of any civilized, democratic nation on the planet.

There should not be any confusion here. The conspiracy is clear and evident for those with eyes to see; but so, too, are the smooth calculations, and numbers do not lie. Some numbers, also, are too shameful to dismiss as chance. Let us take a look at them with open eyes and hearts that unafraid to embrace the ugly truths about ourselves and our country. Only then can we right our footing once again, and keep stepping together through the darkness, fears, and greed into the light of liberation.

Only then can we do what is right as a nation and dismantle mass incarceration.

Before we can crunch these numbers, though, I will ask you to rid yourself of any lofty notions that our prison system's primary goals are to keep society safe and rehabilitate criminals. As the numbers will reflect, our criminal justice system of today is primarily about control and cash, but that doesn't have to be tomorrow's truth...

The vast majority of our obscene prison population consists of non-violent drug offenders. Up until 1982, when Ronald Reagan launched his war on drugs, drug usage had been effectively treated as a public health problem and was actually on the DECLINE! Contrary to what most people think, the leap of our prison population from approximately 300,000 prisoners to 2.3 million had nothing to do with a spike in crime. We did not all of a sudden lose our minds and become a nation of raving criminals.

Drastic changes in our laws are responsible, particularly the addition of the aforementioned mandatory minimums, which increased the length of prison sentences to such a degree that judges literally cried, protested, and retired! One study suggests that the entire increase in the prison population is due to sentencing policy changes.

For example, marijuana, as reported in Ryan King and Marc Mauer's Marijuana: The Transformation of the War on Drugs in the 1990's, is a relatively harmless drug. A 1988 surgeon general's report lists tobacco and alcohol as more dangerous. Yet, marijuana possession accounted for nearly 80% of the growth in drug arrests in the 1990's.

An even more embarrassing example can be found by looking at the extraordinary increase in prison admissions due to parole and probation violations. In 1980, only one percent of prison admissions were due to violations of parole. By 2000, a whopping 35% of those sent to prison were parole violators. The tool worked so well that there were almost as many people returned to prison for parole violations in 2000 as were admitted in 1980 for each and every reason!

The U.S. now has the highest rate of incarceration in the world, even surpassing those of highly repressive regimes, like Russia, China, and Iran. No other country incarcerates as many of its racial or ethnic minorities. The U.S. imprisons a larger percentage of its Black population than South Africa did at the height of apartheid. For all our criticisms of former socialist countries' "labor camps," America has more prisoners working for her than any other nation.

The fact that we need to focus on as Americans is that prisons are not effective in deterring crime nor in reformation of criminals. As John F. Pfaff, author of Locked In: The True Cause of Mass Incarceration and how to Achieve Real Reform, points out on page ten, locking up more people has proven ineffective in dealing with rising crime rates.

For instance, on page twelve of his book, he not only iterates how reducing the state prison population by 4% resulted in a staggering 10% decrease in crime in Pennsylvania, but studies showed that crime fell in almost every state that scaled back incarceration.

We must move beyond the unfounded fears and believe in our fellow citizens enough to tackle the policy pushers and profiteers who are succeeding at the cost of this suffering. As Pfaff covers on page one-hundred and eighty-five, state prisons have become a source of revenue for the very same states who decide the policies that are directly benefiting them financially. A grotesque conflict of interest that guarantees any reforms even will be hard fought. Then we have the unions, the correctional officers, the scores of state and government officials, and all the material and service providers who will scramble to form a united front in defense of their jobs and portions of that $80 billion dollar burden that is largely carried by hard working taxpayers.

With so many people now benefitting, if not dependent upon, mass incarceration, it may be totally unfathomable to some that as recent as the mid-1970's, some of the most well-respected criminologists were predicting a fading away of prisons. In 1973, The National Advisory Commission on Criminal Justice Standards and Goals recommended that no new institutions for adults should be built. Existing ones for juveniles should be closed.

How, then, does our prison population quintuple with an expansion unprecedented in human history? Preservation through transformation, bigotry, hypocrisy, and the loophole—all working together to maintain white control at maximum profit to the ruling elite. This disturbing reality is for reasons that have nothing to do with crime trends; our judicial system has become a highly profitable (to some) machine of social control that must be dismantled, abolished like the great evils before it.

The good news is, we're up for the challenge. We've been here before. Our road to redemption has been lit by other enlightened nations who enacted prison reforms with inspiring results. Results that in some cases cut their prison population almost in half—and crime only declined. But change, must first begin within us!

Weldon Angelos was only twenty-four years old. A record producer in possession of a weapon that he never used or threatened anyone with, and yet a Federal Judge was obligated to sentence him to a fifty-five year mandatory minimum sentence for three marijuana sales!

"The Court believes that to sentence Mr. Angelos to prison for the rest of his life is unjust, cruel, and even irrational," the sentencing judge protested, but had to follow the law. It was cases like this that sent Judge Irving into retirement, and led Judge Weinstein to publicly refuse to take any more drug cases.

A Washington, D.C. mother was sentenced to five years in prison after being convicted of "possession of crack" found by police in a locked box that her son had hidden in her attic. It was after regretfully issuing this mandatory sentence that Judge Marshall told a reporter that it's killing me that I'm sending so many low level offenders away for all this time."

And it was the ten year sentence, without parole, that Judge Schwarzer was forced to slap a first time offender with (an Oakland longshoreman who made the lapse in judgement of giving a drug dealer a ride to a meeting with an undercover agent) that broke him down on the bench.

Leandro Andrade was sentenced to fifty years without parole for stealing children's videotapes from a Kmart. Another man was also sentenced under the controversial three strikes law: twenty-five years to life for stealing three golf clubs from a pro shop. The distinguished Supreme Court Justice David H. Souter hinted that the conviction was cruel and unusual with this quip: "If Andrade's sentence is not grossly dispropriate, the principle has no meaning."

I need not belabor these miscarriages of justices; judges across the land already have. There's not a man nor woman beneath the sun who can't review these cases, look at these numbers, or hear these judge's cries and protests, and understand that something has gone drastically wrong with our judicial system. Not a single one of these people left so much as a scratch on another human being, but each effectively had their lives destroyed by appallingly long, undeserved sentences. These are real people, real cases, and real judges. These are the vast majority of non-violent citizens who make up the fodder of mass incarceration.

Professor Pfaff, on page seven of his book, Locked-In, states that the real political power behind prison growth are the public officials who benefit from large prisons, the politicians in districts with prisons, along with prison guards who staff them, and the public sector unions who represent them. We must unite and stand together with one voice and one vote to tell them, "NO MORE!"

With even a quarter of the $80 billion prisons drain from the economy, new progressive institutions and jobs can easily be created, state by state. Rehabilitation programs outside of prison have been proven to do a much better job of reducing crime. People must build, monitor, and staff these facilities, which will equal more jobs and crime reduction. And, as Pfaff shows on page eighty-eight, Pennsylvania closed two prisons in 2013 and laid off only three guards. Due to drastic prison reforms, the prison population in New York fell by 25% in five years, but they haven't closed any prisons.

We are Americans, the brave and resilient, we can and will find a way!

Between 1960-1990 official crime rates in Finland, Germany, and the U.S. were nearly identical. Yet, the U.S. incarceration rate quadrupled and kept rising. The German rate was stable. The Finnish rate fell by a staggering 60%! You should not need to ask why there was such a disparity between the U.S. and Finnish at this point. The Finnish don't have sixty million ex-slaves, a deplorable "someone must rule" mindstate, and they never created any new systems, tools, or institutions of control.

They did what we must do, what's best for our country as a whole. They maximized what had worked so effectively for us and poured more people and resources into treating drug usage as a public health problem. They decriminalized drugs and taxed its sales; they poured more money into education, rehabilitation, counselling, and job training and job creation. They, in a patriotic essence, chose to invest in the success rather than the failure of their young citizens and country—and all have prospered with crime being at an all-time low.

Our infant nation has suffered through enough long, bloody struggles. The ruling elite's time is up! The prisons and profiteers' time is up! The macho-man's mindstate of "someone must rule" is up! Hypocrisy, bigotry, misogyny, racism, sexism—and yes, mass incarceration's time is up! Dismantling and doing away with this, our latest form of "preservation through transformation" does not start with revolution or riots, movements nor petitions. The very first step we must take is acknowledging that this newest method of social control—the maintaining of a perpetual undercaste and the status quo since 1776—is wrong.

It does not take racial hatred to maintain such diabolical evils as slavery, Jim Crow, and mass incarceration. All it takes is racial indifference by the majority. The second step in shutting down and shedding the shame, therefore, is truly embracing the call of Dr. Martin Luther King to be lovestruck, to care deeply about one another.

Let that love and care be manifested in compassion for each and every individual, including the poor and vulnerable, regardless of race, religion, and sexual orientation.

That love, care, and compassion will demand action! It will demand that we motivate, through our C-4 (Concerned Citizens Contributing to Change) Movement, petitions, protests, votes, that presidential pen once more to completely dismantle mass incarceration. Only then can we begin healing and rebuilding the families and communities that it has destroyed for nearly four decades.

The Finnish have provided a blueprint. Let's live up to our creed and highest principles. Let's prove ourselves to be the home of the brave, as we return to the land of the free, daring to strive to top the Finnish results by reducing our prison population by 70% over the next ten years! Let's follow them into that lofty dream of a minimal-crime society where goodwill is the ruler and the criminal justice system is solely concerned with keeping society safe and rehabilitating criminals.

If we can conceive it, we can achieve it: for we are Americans!

The story of incarceration is not a singular one. Just as the story of marginalization or the dynamics of power do not follow a singular linear moral pathway throughout our history. That is why it is important to broaden the spectrum of voices being held in the great captivity business. Whether free or encaged, we all live with some kind of stigma—that's the nature of making decisions you can't take back. We have to temper our own regret with our belief that our work matters at some deeply philosophical or social level, that cannot be represented by anybody else. So, as a writer, we are conscientious that a sense of self-value can only be created personally. If we are looking to be redeemed at some greater social level with our work, I'd say that is an undue expectation for our art. We only get short windows of time on this earth to be and create, wasting it because we want other people to love or like, or forgive us is a lot of pressure to put on our art.

— Zeke Caligiuri
2011-2015, Multi-Prize winner in Poetry, Fiction and Memoir,
PEN America Prison Writing Awards

2019 PEN AMERICA PRISON WRITING AWARDS IN **DRAMA**

I really have no expectations [for my reception in literary community.] It's more "casting bread upon the waters" than expecting some acclamation. I've submitted works that I thought were the pinnacles of my abilities, that were ignored, baffling me, then received national writing awards for works that didn't impress me at all. My hopes are that I can continue to "bear witness" and express the truth about my experiences, communicating those truths to those "out there," who would not otherwise conceive of the realities we live through. When a prison guard read one of my poems, she said, shivering, "It gave me goosebumps, it made me cry," that may have been the highest praise I'd received.

— Charles Norman

First Prize, Drama

The Thaw
DEREK TRUMBO

CHARACTERS Young'un, twenties; Old Man, fifties; Edwin, thirties

SETTING The play is set in a 10x15 foot concrete cell, the cell shared by the prisoners housed within. Two bunkbeds, several chairs, and lockers make up the majority of the cell. Also included, almost as an afterthought, is an unused table with scattered debris, and the remains of chopped pills set atop it. There is a big set of double windows at the back, covered in sheets. There are numerous items scattered on the floor, the remains of a ransacking that took place earlier. Papers and books, clothes and food wrappers litter the floor.

AT RISE Edwin lays in the bottom bunk of one of the bunkbeds, he is still and rarely moves. Young'un sits on a chair center stage as old Man, paces back and forth to keep warm. It is the dead of winter, and the cell is extremely cold. The time is present.

Lights Up.

OLD MAN

You had to have something you wanted from life before you came to prison.

YOUNG'UN

You talk too much. And I know you're freezing because I sure am, Now quiet down before you wake Edwin up.

OLD MAN

What difference does it make? It's good to talk, talking keeps everything from... Why didn't you stand up for yourself? You've been here a little more than 5 months, and you're already someone's prison wife. Is that what you envisioned when the judge gave you your sentence? Being a prison wife?

YOUNG'UN

You think you have it all figured out.

OLD MAN

What's to figure out? I live in the same 10x15 square as you bubba. I see everything you and your douchebag buddy are up to. I can't help but to.

YOUNG'UN

Do you wanna get smacked again? Edwin's always looking for an excuse to smack the shit out of you.

OLD MAN

Is that why you let him do what he does?

YOUNG'UN

If he hears you... I'm not giving you your cover back, if that's where you're trying to take it.

OLD MAN

Why, you scared he's going to beat us both?

YOUNG'UN

Could you stop him?

OLD MAN

Would you even attempt to?

YOUNG'UN

I'm not talking about that... Aren't you cold?

OLD MAN

Why, you going to give me my cover back?

YOUNG'UN

You know how mad he'd be.

OLD MAN

Fuck Edwin.

YOUNG'UN

(Whispers.) If you wake him...

OLD MAN

Do I look like I'm scared?

YOUNG'UN

You look cold, and old. Like an old shoe left out in the snow. An old boot.

OLD MAN

Look, just for the sake of conversation.

YOUNG'UN

He's gonna smack the holy hell outta both of us if we wake him.

OLD MAN

He ain't going to do shit to me. Now as I was saying, is this—this right here—freezing your sweet-little-ass off what you expected from life five years ago? Two years ago? Yesterday? Better yet, is it what you expected when you let him talk you into knocking all the damn glass out of our windows? Well?

YOUNG'UN

Shut up.

OLD MAN

Or what?

YOUNG'UN

Do you see any-DAMN-body else giving a damn what I do?
(Glances nervously at Edwin, who moves a bit.)

OLD MAN

Nervous much?

YOUNG'UN

You're just as scared of him as I am.

OLD MAN

And that's what makes me speak up. That's why I complain, and
nag, and — (Louder) point out all the stupid shit!

YOUNG'UN

(Nervously glancing at Edwin.) I'm not gonna pull him offa you this
time.

OLD MAN

Don't you get it? LOOK AT HIM! He's so high he's not even in the
room with us right now. Look here, Young'un, you really should get
up, move around, get that blood of yours circulating.

YOUNG'UN

Why do you care? Why are you always sticking your damn nose in
my business?

OLD MAN

Because I'm old. That's why. Once you get past a certain age, you
stop wondering what the fuck you keep stepping in, and recognize it
for what it is: Somebody else's shit. How can I keep myself out?

YOUNG'UN

You knew they weren't gonna fix the windows.

OLD MAN

Possibly.

YOUNG'UN

And that it was gonna get cold.

OLD MAN

Call 'em seasons for a reason.

YOUNG'UN

And you let me bust them out anyway.

OLD MAN

Ain't my windows. They the state's damn windows.

YOUNG'UN

So you don't give a shit is what you're saying?

OLD MAN

Young'un, it don't matter to me whether it's hotter than the blue blazes or colder than a well digger's ass, I'm always cold. You either adapt or die. Easy as that.

YOUNG'UN

Adapt then old man, I'm the one with the blankets.

OLD MAN

Yup.

YOUNG'UN

You're about an ornery-assed old man. Look at you. What've you got, a set of thermals, and some sweats-?

OLD MAN

Don't forget the compression socks. Mustn't do that.

YOUNG'UN

For all your piss and vinegar, you're nothing but an old pushover, I took your blanket, and you let me.

OLD MAN

Yup.

YOUNG'UN

Nothing but a bitch, same as me. Just another bitch trying not to make waves.

OLD MAN

Yup. Swimming against an ocean of shit. Sounds just about right. Those currents can be treacherous.

YOUNG'UN

Fuck it's cold. (Yawns.) I'm so tired I could sleep until count time. (Gazes at Edwin.)

OLD MAN

Let me show you something.

YOUNG'UN

I'm so tired I feel like taking them frozen-assed sheets down from the windows, and using them to make my damn bed up. A man can only wake up with his face stuck to his cold mat like it's a slobbercicle so many times before it gets to be too much. When the officers come in for count time, tell 'em to write me up or count me in my damn rack. Fuck count time.

OLD MAN

I've got a few shots of coffee, some jalapenos and a bag of red hots you and your prison daddy didn't manage to find when you were rooting around in my shit as usual.

YOUNG'UN

And you're telling me why?

OLD MAN

Because if you eat hot shit it gets the old blood heated up. What the fuck you mean.

YOUNG'UN

So that's your secret? You're not cold cause of red hots?

OLD MAN

The damn hiding spot's the secret, genius. The coffee and shit's just good old fashioned common sense.

YOUNG'UN

Edwin's gonna know about this. You know I can't keep nothing from him.

OLD MAN

That's your own fault. What you need is to learn how to stand up for yourself.

YOUNG'UN

You seen what happened the last time.

OLD MAN

Beat your ass, broke your spirit, and turned you into something you're not. Yet you still tell him you love him. Yeah, I saw.

YOUNG'UN

You don't know what it's like.

OLD MAN

Don't I? You don't do as much time as I have without growing lonely... and adapting.

YOUNG'UN

How 'bout you just come off them red hots.

OLD MAN

First the coffee. (Fixes a cup, gives it to him.) Sip, don't chug. Feel the caffeine? Drink it.

YOUNG'UN

Why are you being nice to me?

OLD MAN

Because we ain't being pitted against each other for a change.

YOUNG'UN

That's not what... It's just his way is all... You remind him of his dad... That's why.

OLD MAN

Every damn swinging dick in this place has family issues.

YOUNG'UN

He loves me.

OLD MAN

I just bet he does.

YOUNG'UN

Sometimes you just wanna feel... good for a change... you know?

OLD MAN

I had a boy once, Young, outgoing, charming, and an ass like greek marble. Not a hair on his ass or legs. And when we kissed. Let's just say I ain't never had someone who could make my knees weak, rod hard, and head swim all at the same damn time, Yeah, I know what it's like.

YOUNG'UN

What happened?

OLD MAN

I stopped being what he needed me to be. The cold set in, and it got harder to thaw the old blood. Even the world's best kisser can't miracles make. In time both the rod and the back bend with the weight of age.

YOUNG'UN

He left you. Wow. Thanks for the sob story.

OLD MAN

My baby... He got sick, I loved him so much I followed him all the
way to the last stop... Hospice care. I held his hand...

YOUNG'UN

Yeah, that's a shame. We're clean.

OLD MAN

You ready for them jalapenos?

YOUNG'UN

Let me finish this cold ass coffee.

OLD MAN

Shouldn't have broke my hot pot. Now, eat one, then sip the juice.
Eat, sip, eat, sip. And walk around while you do it.

YOUNG'UN

I'm good.

OLD MAN

Do it, or no red hots.

YOUNG'UN

Fine. (Walks and eats.)

OLD MAN

So, how'd you like them Lortabs?

YOUNG'UN

I didn't. I don't know shit about pills.

OLD MAN

Mum-hmm. (Sits, relaxes.)

YOUNG'UN

Remember when Edwin got that wild idea of squirting out all
Jaime's inhaler, and drying it out until the mist crystalized and he
could snort it? That's what gave him the urge to get into your meds.

OLD MAN

Mmm-hmm. I sort of figured that out.

YOUNG'UN

If you hadn't complained about all the pain—

OLD MAN

Edwin's a piece of shit.

YOUNG'UN

He said you were dying... I'm wearing two covers, why am I still cold?

OLD MAN

That would be because Edwin wouldn't know a Lortab 10 from a hole in his ass.

YOUNG'UN

Those weren't pain pills were they?

OLD MAN

Nope. You and your dumbass prison daddy just got finished snorting nearly an entire months worth of my diabetes medication.

YOUNG'UN

We what?

OLD MAN

That's why you're cold. Your blood sugar has crashed, heart rate's slowing, and that tired sluggish feeling washing over you is your body's way of telling you just how bad you've fucked up. Consider it a hibernation you'll never wake from.

YOUNG'UN

Edwin! (Pulls back the covers, Edwin isn't moving.) He... he's not...

OLD MAN

He's not going to be needing those blankets.

YOUNG'UN

You... you knew.

OLD MAN

Ready for them red hots?

YOUNG'UN

He's gonna die.

OLD MAN

Who you going to save, him or you?

YOUNG'UN

I... I think I'm ready for those red hots.

OLD MAN

Figured you would be. Used to be my favorite when I was your age, before prison. Yeah, how about you come over here and get you some feel good. How's that sound?

YOUNG'UN

(Takes the candy, paces as he eats.) Count time's coming, them Cos gonna know what's happened. They'll say we killed him once they notice Edwin's not-

OLD MAN

Listen to me son... You're going to need those blankets he's got.

YOUNG'UN

(Throws off his covers.) I'll just freeze with him. That's what I'll do. I'll flip a coin, leave it to fate.

OLD MAN

(Laughs) Ha! Ha-ahhh... Been pissing blood for a month or three, Too damn stubborn to get myself checked out. Figured if they ain't caught it by my B-day I'd just take it as a sign. Mmm-hmm.

YOUNG'UN

When's your birthday?

OLD MAN

Six months ago... Right before you got here.

YOUNG'UN

I don't think I can make it to count time...

(Paces, lost in thought.)

Old Man begins to clean the cell.

OLD MAN

I called my boy Muffin... No, everybody else called him that... I called him... I used to clean up after him too... He was such a stinker... I miss him.

YOUNG'UN

The sheets! All this time it's been the sheets —

(He looks at the window, and forms an idea.)

OLD MAN

I called him my Sunshine. All those years and I never once told him... I couldn't allow myself to... Everyone knew what we were. What he meant to me. And that didn't... I sat there holding his hand, and couldn't say it. Mmm-hmmm.

YOUNG'UN

(Tears the sheets from the window.) Don't you see? Everyone forgot we knocked the windows out. The Cos saw the sheets, and truth be told, couldn't care less why it was so cold in here. They knew we knocked them out during the heatwave and- Don't you see? They will come in at count time and see the windows out and —

OLD MAN

Mum-hmm.

YOUNG'UN

When they ask what happened? I'll tell them. I'll tell them everything. I'll say Edwin. That's what I'll say. Edwin happened.

174

OLD MAN

Mmmm...

YOUNG'UN

And come spring—I always wanted to jog. You know? I wanted
to—Come spring I'm gonna take up fucking jogging. Then running.
Maybe I'll just start out chasing people. I'll run as far, and as fast as I
can, and folks will say I'm chasing the devil. You hear me old Man?
I'll run just for the hell of it.

To hell what anybody thinks... Is that crazy?

OLD MAN

...

YOUNG'UN

(Checks on him, no response. Young'un takes Edwin's blankets,
and covers the old man. He sits beside him and holds the old man's
hand.) I know I'm probably talking too much, but I'm gonna be a
runner. You'll be so proud of me. You'll see. Just as soon as spring
comes, Mmm-hmm.

THE END

Second Prize, Drama

Time
ASHLEY STARLING THOMAS

CHARACTERS

CHI: Early Thirties, African American, in year ten of a forty five year
drug conspiracy sentence. Strives to live by her own moral code and
doesn't trust the system.

KAYLA: Mid-twenties, Caucasian, a recovering drug addict, serving
a four month sentence for trafficking illegals. Naïve to the prison
world, always sees the good in people and searching for a friend.

GUARD: Man, late forties, indifferent to system. Works for the
prison because he couldn't get a job anywhere else and only there to
collect a check.

SETTING

A two man prison hold-over cell, during the time of mass
incarceration in America.

PROLOGUE:

Sometime in the Millennial.

The lights come up as Chi sits quietly in the cell reading over her legal paperwork, humming and rapping to a beat inside her head. Chi is a stunning woman who has become a hardened prisoner and believes the system is meant to keep all Black people captive. She's been handed down a forty-five year sentence for conspiracy to sell crack cocaine. Her family has deserted her and she has no one but herself. Chi has been waiting for the United States marshalls to pick her up for two months. Chi has made the cell her home and hopes they will come and pick her up any day to take her to her designated prison. Her hair is braided back and she wears her prison attire extra baggie. Her diction is crisp, and she is educated.

ACT I

CHI: Raps: They say history repeats itself, I say we were slaves then, we're slaves now, they just rearranged us on the shelf, I was birthed into a system designed to fail. Will I ever find success? Only this time will tell. I remember when I was a young girl, writing letters to my momma and my daddy in jail. Who knew back then that I was up next in the cell?

CHI stops and thinks about her words.

CHI: raps: A repetitious cycle from generation to generation I guess it's to be expected when you're Black and living in the most incarcerated nation.

A loud buzzing sound.

(The Guard and Kayla enter and stand of front of the cell.)

GUARD: Open cell 11.

Kayla, a frail woman with blonde hair and bright blue eyes stands at the cell door holding her bed cot and jail clothes in her hand.

Chi doesn't turn around and look. She keeps nodding her head to her own beat.

A loud buzzing sound and the cell door closes.

Kayla looks around, disturbed by her new atmosphere.

KAYLA: I'm Kayla, I just got here.

CHI: I don't care who you are. Don't bother me and I won't bother you. Stay on your side and I'll stay on my side and we won't have no problems. That's your side right there.

(Chi points to Kayla's bunk)

(Kayla looks and puts her things down)

CHI: Make sure your bed is inspection ready by 7am.

KAYLA: What does inspection ready mean?

(Chi looks at Kayla then gets up)

CHI: Don't tell me this your first time being locked up. Damn! Why they always wanna give me the new ones? Look, I'm not your friend. I don't care about your problems and I damn sure don't care to get to know you. I'm not your babysitter or you're prison mom, cousin or sister. Understand? I'm a tell you these rules one time and one time only. You don't get it; that's on you. Breakfast is at six, lunch is at nine and dinner is at three. We count three times a day. They set up rules and then don't want to follow them themselves. I don't talk to the police so if you do you might as well get asked to move right now 'cause I don't tolerate snitches. Understand? Shop day is on Wednesday if you get money and don't expect me to give you anything. Y'all never did nothing for us but take from my people so I don't expect no handouts either.

(Kayla bursts into tears)

CHI: Oh, hell naw! We not gone have that! Nope, no, no, no, no, no! Why are you crying? There ain't no crying in this cell. Dry them tears up, right now!

(Kayla continues to sob uncontrollably)

CHI: I'm not gone deal with this. Guard! Guard! Guard!

(The Guard doesn't answer)

CHI: Every time! Why can't I ever just get a cell mate who can do time!

KAYLA: I'm sorry. I just — I just — it's hard for me.

CHI: And you don't think it's hard for me?

KAYLA: I'm not saying that, but I don't know how I am going to get through this. Away from my family and friends, and my daughter — she needs me. It's my fault. It's all my fault.

(Kayla cries again)

CHI: Stop crying. Stop crying. (Yells) Stop crying! Damn! (Chi sits on her bunk) How much time you got?

KAYLA: (Wipes her tears) Four months. I got four months. I got four months for trafficking illegals across the border. I don't know why I even did it. I need the money and it seemed like a good opportunity at the time. Just a little extra cash in my pocket to pay my bills and buy my daughter some school clothes. I'm here just because I needed a little extra money.

CHI: We all in here for just a little extra money. The kingpins snitch and they get less time. They rat on the little people and the prosecutor shows them favor. But what I am supposed to say when I don't know nothing. He didn't tell me nothing. What am I supposed to say? Make up names, make up lies, like he did, frame my own people just to take the heat off of me? He's already home now, living his life in his happy little house and I'm here, left to rot away by a capitalistic system that throws my people in the death chamber every time they get the chance with conspiracy. They are the conspiracy. They don't know everything. They're not God. They try to play God but they're not God. The crack laws were made to repress us, to hold us down and throw us under the jail cell. They flood the black community with crack, then sentence 100 to 1 versus cocaine. That's because cocaine is the white man's drug. We can't afford it, it's too expensive. And then they're mad because I went to trial. Isn't that crazy? I get punished for my constitutional right, for them to actually do their job and bear the burden of proof. I get punished. I wasn't signing no deal for something I didn't do. Nope, no, I'm a do my time. I'ma do it. They can lock my body up but they can't cage my mind. I'm still free. Just cause you're locked up don't mean you can't be free. I'm still free.

KAYLA: I tried crack once I didn't like it. Heroin was my drug of choice. Made me forget about all the bad things that happened in my life.

CHI: Only reason why they trying to change the laws now is because it's affecting the white people. That meth is a hell of a drug and it's everywhere, all through the trailer parks and suburbs. That's the only reason they care now. Because it's their children getting hit with five and ten years bids. Oh, now it's a problem? Now it's an American epidemic!

KAYLA: How much time did they give you?

CHI: Forty-five years.

(The Guard enters and walks by the cell)

GUARD: Lights out! You inmates can talk tomorrow.

The lights fade out on the cell. Kayla and Chi lay down in there bed in silence. Kayla begins to cry again.

ACT II

The lights come up on the cell. KAYLA is sitting in the bed with her knees to her chest, rocking back and forth, staring off into space. Her heroin withdrawal has kept her up all night. CHI is eating food off of a tray. Kayla's tray is sitting untouched on the small table. CHI looks over at Kayla and shakes her head and continues to eat.

CHI: You not gonna eat that?

KAYLA: I'm not hungry.

CHI: (Takes tray) You gone have to eat something. Starving yourself is going to get you put in seg.

KAYLA: What is seg?

CHI: Segregation, the SHU, special housing unit. It's where they put the crazies and the snitches.

KAYLA: I'm not crazy and I'm not a snitch. I'm just not hungry.

CHI: Why were you shaking in your sleep last night? I almost punched you, I thought somebody was in here last night the way you were flopping around like a fish and screaming like you had a demon in you. What's wrong with you?

KAYLA: The medicine I take gives me bad nightmares and I'm still withdrawing for heroin.

CHI: Why do you all do that?

KAYLA: Do what?

CHI: Put that poison in your body? I don't understand if a drug makes you sick just come off of it what's the point? Don't you do drugs to make you feel better, not worse?

KAYLA: You never did drugs before?

CHI: No, and I never plan on it.

KAYLA: But you are here for drugs right?

CHI: No, I'm here for conspiracy to sell crack cocaine and because I wouldn't snitch out my boyfriend's family. Conspiracy is the easiest thing for the feds to get you on because they don't have to prove anything. All they gotta do is get one person, an informant or a snitch to say they saw you sell drugs or heard from somebody that you sold them drugs and they can convict you. I never touched crack a day in my life. I was scared of it. My daddy was addicted my whole life and I saw what he did to get it. I never wanted to be him but growing up where I came from selling dope is the normal way of life. It's like selling tires and people always need tires. I knew my boyfriend sold it, but I didn't think it would affect me. I didn't think I would come to prison for him selling drugs. I was in school, I wanted better, I wanted out of the hood, out of the life. But how was I supposed to do that without money to pay for my books, or to keep a roof over my head? It's an oxymoron to be Black and try to live the American life. Go to school, get educated, then you'll get a better job, a better life. You can move into the neighbored where the police don't roam the streets harassing everybody, a place where you don't get killed for just walking home from the bus stop from a dude up the street or a racist pig cop, mad cause his daughter likes black boys.

I tried to do right, do the opposite of what I witnessed every day, tried to be different, and I still ended up in prison. I still fell victim to the game, to the system.

KAYLA: We didn't have money either.

CHI: But you're white. It's different. It's better to be a poor white than a poor black in today's society. The system is designed for us to fail.

KAYLA: (starts to cry) I don't know how I am going to make it. It's so hard. Oh, God I can't do this, I can't do this.

CHI: Aw c'mon, here we go again with the tears. Those tears didn't stop the judge from sentencing you to prison. You go home in less than one hundred and twenty days. How can you cry about that? I would sleep a hundred and twenty days. A hundred and twenty days and a wake-up.

KAYLA: But you don't understand. I don't have that kind of time.

CHI: I don't understand? You can see the end of the tunnel, the light, it's there right there for you. If I don't get an appeal or a law passes, I will die in this place. Time, you want to talk about time? You stand in the courtroom and hear a judge tell you forty-five years for something you didn't do. He might as well say you're Black and your life doesn't matter so do this time and make the best of it.

CHI: Another black person off the streets, one less crack baby we gotta worry about on the streets robbing the good white ladies for their purses. The prosecutors, the attorneys, the judge all of them, in cahoots. And after they're done railroading you up state or to the feds, they all go have lunch and discuss their menial lives over a cocktails in an expensive country club

KAYLA: Not every white person is racist. I'm not racist. I got Black friends, Mexicans..

CHI: You're missing the point. I know that everyone is not racist, I'm not racist. I love all people. This country is racist, a systemic oppressive device to control and manipulate the minds of its inhabitants. They flash the lifestyles of the rich and famous on TV, giving us false hope that one day we can all be rich but not if you live in the hood. The only way to get money in the hood is to sell drugs but in the white school, they get the best of everything. They make you want to go to school and learn, they make the atmosphere conducive to learning. It's deeper than you can imagine. Think, Kayla, think. Have you ever asked yourself why child molesters get less time than drug dealers, or why there are more minorities in prison when we account for less of the population in America?

KAYLA: No, I guess not.

CHI: That's because you never had to. I've been in a cell with a woman who let random men see naked photos of her two year old daughter. Do you know how much time she got? Seven years. Seven. Damn. Years. She'll do five, get out and live her life while her daughter is left to fend for herself in a system that doesn't give a damn about her.

KAYLA: I never looked at it that way. I would never do that to my daughter. I hate people who touch on innocent kids. You can't blame drugs for that, that's just wrong.

CHI: You cry about four months, you'll be home with your daughter doing whatever you want while I'm stuck here a slave to the system, a slave, a new slave with my master's degree, working for free, living in a cell, eating slops, just hoping one day that I'll get some crumbs to survive. My mama used to always say, "Let him who have wisdom understand" but they don't understand. They'll never understand how it feels to try and do everything right, the way they want and still end up in a cage. I'm not going to let this time break me. No matter what I'll do my time how I want to do my time.

KAYLA: (coughs hard and throws up blood)

CHI: Are you okay?

KAYLA: Yea, I'm okay. It's the medicine. I've been trying to get the one I got on the outside but they told me they don't carry that here so they gave me one like it. I guess it's okay. I'll just have to deal with it.

(The GUARD enters)

CHI: Guard, can she get some help. She's throwing up blood.

GUARD: It's officer to you, inmate, and that's not my job description. Put a cop-out into medical. She looks fine to me.

CHI: Tell me what is your job description?

GUARD: Not to be wiping up blood.

(The Guard exits)

KAYLA: (lies back on the bed) Oh, God. I don't know if I can do this. I'm ready to go home. Sorry, I didn't mean to rub it in your face.

CHI: You're good. These guards are slaves too, they just don't know it, slaves to the system that controls their livelihood. Every day, waking up to counting down the days until they retire. What kind of life is that? A meaningless one, with no identity.

KAYLA: Maybe his wife left him. I would have, look at him--all mean and angry.

CHI: Do you know why they call us inmates?

KAYLA: Because we are prisoners, in prison.

CHI: No, because we are in an insane asylum. Society labels us mentally deranged with social intelligence issues if we can't follow their man made laws. Something must be wrong with us mentally to veer off from the path that society has laid out for us. Welcome to America where there are no prisoners or prisons. The prisons are called correctional institutions or reform camps that resemble more like concentration camps. Our identity stripped from us, labeled convicts, given a new name and branded with a number. It's all a part of their game to try and brain wash us. It's a money game too. The more inmates they get the fatter their pockets grow. It's a corporation where we, the humans, are the stock.

There are three types of inmates. One, the one who thinks this place is reforming them, becomes friends with the authority, the ones who are oppressing them; two the one who manipulates the system and acts like they want them to act in order to gain rank or position in the prison, and three, the one who completely goes against everything the establishment stands for and gets punished severely for it. I'm three. I know these prisons are not for reform, they don't want to help us, they want to make money off us and keep us in bondage. I'm a political prisoner, here because I won't conform to what they want me to be. What are you Kayla? What kind of inmate are you?

GUARD: (yells off screen) Lights out!

KAYLA: I don't know.

The lights fade out as Kayla ponders on Chi's questions.

ACT III

The lights come up on the Chi in the cell. Kayla's bunk is empty. Chi wakes up and looks over at the empty bunk. Chi stands up and looks around. Kayla's uneaten tray is sitting on the desk. Chi takes a bite of the bread.

(The Guard enters)

GUARD: Inmate, roll up this bed. CHI: Why? Where is Kayla? What happened to Kayla?

GUARD: The one that was here? Oh, (chuckles) she died last night.

CHI: How? How did she die?

GUARD: I don't know. They said cancer or something like that. Now roll up this bed I got another inmate coming in.

(The Guard exits)

Chi stands there contemplating, looking up to the sky.

A ticking tock is heard as the lights fade out on cell 11.

Third Prize, Drama

I'm Here for You
LARRY STROMBERG

On the stage is Old Louey. Old Louey is 85 years old; he is bald, suffering from Alzheimer's disease, and facing progressive loss of mental capacity. Old Louey sits in a chair staring into space. He holds a walking cane in his right hand. The cane moves back and forth from Old Louey's shaking hands.

There is silence on the stage as Old Louey sits there. His lack of facial expression makes him look almost lifeless. Old Louey's oldest son enters from stage left. His name is Joey and he's in his early fifties. Joey is visiting his father for the first time in years, and he's unprepared for the extent of Old Louey's deterioration. Joey slowly walks over to his father, trying to hold back his tears.

JOEY: I'm here for you. (Pause) I'm here. (Beat) I'm gonna stay with you this time. I'm not going away anymore. I'm here, Pop. (Beat) Here to stay...

(Joey looks closely at his father, lovingly.)

JOEY: I'm sorry for letting you down, Pop. For letting our whole family down. For letting Jenna and the kids down. (Beat) For letting myself down.

(Tears begin to flow from Joey's eyes.)

JOEY: You always had my best interest at heart, Pop. You wanted me to take over the family business. This was a dream you had for me. You built the business from the ground up. With blood, sweat and a few bucks in your pocket. I admire you for that, Pop. The business was a gift you wanted to give me. I spit in your face! I was so strung out, man. I screwed the hell up. Just like I did with everything else in my life. I'm a piece of total crap! Let's face the damn truth here. I let you down, Pop. I'm so sorry, Pop. My regret is as deep as the deep blue seas. My sorrow is endless. It's the cross I must bear, Pop. (Beat) I should have been here for you and the whole family. For Jenna and the kids! I failed you all. You all depended on me.

(Joey takes a step forward in his grief.)

JOEY: Hell, I couldn't even depend on myself. I couldn't even trust myself. (Beat) I wanted to do the right thing. I swear I did. (Beat) But I always did the opposite.

(Joey turns towards his father. Old Louey just looks on with lifeless eyes.)

JOEY: I didn't want to hurt you, Pop. I didn't want to hurt anybody. (Pause) I destroyed all of my dreams. They're all gone, Pop. (Beat) All gone. I had everything handed to me on a golden plate. A full scholarship to Ohio State. It was right there in my grasp.

(Joey looks at his hands and clenches his fists.)

JOEY: It was right there and I wasted it.

(Joey lowers his hands in defeat.)

JOEY: It made me feel so important to look into your eyes and see how proud you were of me

(Joey steps back and looks into his father's eyes.)

JOEY: What do you see now, Pop? Do you see your son? A junkie? A murderer? (Beat) What do you see? Can you see me at all? (Beat) Can you, Pop?

(Joey looks forward, remembering a grand day long ago.)

JOEY: You taught me to be a great running back, from Pop Warner through high school. I wanted to be just like you. You were a running back in your football days. You are my hero, Pop. (Beat) You always pushed me to be the best that I could be. To be tough. Strong with no fear. To run with the fury. (Pause) Nobody could outrun me in wind sprints. I was the fastest. You built me an awesome gym at the house. We worked out hard together, man. Nobody could out-bench press, squat, shoulder press and deadlift me. Nobody, man. (Pause) All the girls wanted to go out with me. I loved it.

(Joey smiles.)

JOEY: You were at every practice, Pop. Remember?

(Old Louey looks on with the eyes of a doll.)

JOEY: I miss your encouragement. How you cheered me on at every game.

(Joey paces to the other side of his father.)

JOEY: Do you remember that game against Ridley High, Pop? Huh? (Beat) I'll never forget it. The snow was coming down so thick. I couldn't see the scoreboard or even my breath. There was no visibility. But I knew there was only five seconds left on the game clock. Ridley was up on us (21-17) and I wanted the ball. Even in the thick snow, your image stood out, standing in the stands. I heard you yell out; "Run with the fury, Joey." This gave me the inspiration even more, Pop. There was no stopping me. They fed me the ball and I rushed through an open gap and ran it in for the win. That game was for State Champions! It was the greatest day of my life, Pop! You were so proud of me.

(Joey looks at his father.)

JOEY: It was an honor to give you the game ball, Pop. It was the greatest day of my life. We shared it together.
Some things we never forget. I hope you didn't forget, Pop.

(Old Louey stares into space. Sorrow appears back on Joey's face)

JOEY: Don't worry about nothing, Pop.

(Joey steps back towards Old Louey and places his hand on his father's shoulder very gently.)

Everything is gonna be okay. I promise you this, Pop. (Pause) I'm clean now and doing good with my recovery. I'm attending a program called "Celebrate Recovery" every week. It's a good program. I'm drug free and I'm gonna stay that way. (Pause) Jenna and the kids are safe. I'll never hurt them again. They forgive me, Pop.

(Joey breaks down in tears.)

JOEY: They want me back home, Pop. After all these years. They love and forgive me, I'm so grateful. (Beat) Mama is okay, Pop. She loves you so much. Frankie and Tina love you too.

(Suddenly, Old Louey stands up in a frenzy, yelling and screaming. His hands shake out of control.)

Old Louey: (Screaming) The ocean blue!!!!

(The cane shifts back and forth with violent force in Old Louey's right hand.)

Old Louey: (Screaming) Blue skies and the endless sea of misery!!!

(Answer = barely 5 mins)

JOEY: Take it easy, Pop! Take it easy!

(Old Louey screams louder.)

Old Louey: The wind will fly you away!!! Away you go!!!

JOEY: Relax, Pop!!!

Old Louey: UP and away!!!

(Joey slowly sits his father down.)

JOEY: Rest, Pop. Don't worry about nothing. I'm here.

Old Louey: The darkness is coming...coming to take us away!

JOEY: I'm here, Pop. I'm here for my second chance. The prodigal son is home.

(Old Louey calms down and stares into space.)

JOEY: I'm standing by your side, Pop. I'm the man you always wanted me to be now.

(Joey looks at his father with sadness in his eyes.)

JOEY: I hope you hear me. (Pause) I'm sorry for not listening to you. You gave me such sound advice. I was so damn prideful. So stupid. I disagreed with you, Mama, and our whole family. When I got Jenna pregnant, I thought my football days were over. You told me to be a man of responsibility. Be a good husband and a good father.

(Joey speaks on to his father. Old Louey's eyes are motionless.)

JOEY: You told me that I could have a family and still go to college and play ball. I could have both. That you would stand by my side.

(Joey starts to break down again.)

JOEY: I wanted both, Pop. I truly did. (Beat) I couldn't take the pressure. Going to school; keeping my grades up; football, and then having a family. A wife and twins. How could I handle all of this, huh? Being a husband and father took away from my dreams Pop. That's how crazy was my thinking. (Beat) I love Jeena and the kids. I do. (Beat) Keeping my grades up was killing me too. Football wasn't fun anymore. It became work. Demanding. (Beat) Everything in life became demanding, Pop. You were demanding.

(Old Louey stares into the unknown.)

JOEY: I needed something to take the edge off. Heroin did that for me. (Pause) I turned to drugs. I became a junkie. A damn addict; who would do anything to get high. (Pause) Then my whole world was turned inside out.

(Joey cries.)

JOEY: I hurt Jenna, Pop. You tried to help me. (Beat) I didn't want anyone's help. I just needed a fix, man. (Beat) I'm sorry I hurt you, Pop. I went crazy; right in front of our whole family and I hit you. Broke your jaw. (Beat) I'm so damn sorry, Pop. Please forgive me. You're my hero, Pop. My hero. I can't take it back. I can't change that day. (Beat) I'm still your son, Pop. I'm your son.

(Joey wipes the tears from his eyes.)

JOEY: I was so ashamed for what I did to you and our family. For what I did to Jenna and the kids. The way I yelled and screamed like a maniac! The violent outbursts! I was in the abyss, Pop. (Beat) My addictions and mental health issues had me in complete darkness. (Beat) I was on the chaotic road of destruction,

(Joey looks forward as sorrow overwhelms him.)

JOEY: I killed a man to feed my addiction, Pop. (Pause) I took his life for only fifty freaking bucks.

(Joey breaks down even more.)

JOEY: I took his life, Pop. (Beat) This man had a family. There were people who adored him. They depended on him. (Pause) He was loved just like I was loved. I killed this man. He was a good person.

(Tears flow from Joey's eyes.)

JOEY: My sorrow is endless, Pop. I'm so sorry. I was so selfish. So lost, man. (Pause) That day I destroyed many lives. This man's family and my family. (Beat) You were so ashamed of me. You didn't even show up for the trial, Pop.

(Joey looks at his father with regret.)

JOEY: One day you stood high in the stands cheering me on, (Beat) Then one day I wasn't your son anymore for what I'd done. You were nowhere to be found. I was a disgrace

(Joey cries.)

JOEY: I heard Mr. Turner's family speak of the agony that I caused them. The tremendous loss that they suffered. The hate they had for me. (Beat) I hated myself. I told them how sorry I was. (Pause) The jury found me guilty and I ended up with a sentence of 20 to 40 years for what I'd done.

(Joey looks forward again.)

JOEY: It was my fall. My fall from grace.

(Joey steps behind his father.)

JOEY: When I killed this innocent man, it broke your heart. Coming to prison broke your heart. Destroying my life, my family, my dreams broke your heart.. This breaks my heart, Pop.

(Joey is still as he looks at his father, wiping his tears.)

JOEY: I'm here now, Pop. I really love you; I need to make this right between us. I'm never gonna let you down again. I promise. (Beat) You never came up with Mama to visit me behind bars. I know you were ashamed of me. I know, Pop. I understand. I do, Pop. (Pause) After all these years in the penitentiary, I'm here now. I'm never gonna let you down again, Pop, I promise you this.

(Joey places his hand on his shoulder again.)

JOEY: Forgive me, Pop. I need you to forgive me. (Pause) I want you to be proud of me. I know when I destroyed my dreams, it destroyed your dreams.

JOEY: I'm a better man now. I got an education in prison. I learned a few trades and gained faith in the Lord, Pop. I took many drug and alcohol programs to deal with my addictions and mental health issues. I'm attending good programs now every week. I'm on a straight path. Jenna and kids have accepted me back into their lives fully, Pop. I'm trying to make things right. Mr. Turner's family has forgiven me now; after all these years they have chosen to forgive me, Pop.

(Joey removes his hand from his father's shoulder.)

JOEY: I'm not a failure, Pop. I'm gonna make it. Please forgive me. I need you to forgive me, Pop. (Beat) Please forgive me.

(Old Louey sits, almost lifeless; Joey looks at his father, hoping for a response.)

JOEY: I know you can hear me. You're stronger than this, Pop. I know you can hear me.

(Joey raises his voice.)

JOEY: (Aggressively) You're stronger than this! You were bigger than life, Pop! You pushed me and said I can do anything in this life. I can do anything. Be anything! Anything I wanted to be! You said, "All you need is to work hard and have faith!" Remember telling me that, Pop? Huh? Well, I'm telling you the same! You can beat this, Pop! You're strong! You are!

(Joey's sorrow is immense, as he looks at his father's frozen face with no response. Joey wipes the tears from his eyes.)

JOEY: Do you remember this, Pop? This song?

(Joey slowly begins to sing softly to his father.)

JOEY: (Sings) I'm here for you/you're never alone. I'm here for you/ you're never alone. I'm here for you/you're never alone. You're never alone/you're never alone. I'm here for you/you're never alone.

(Joey sings with heavy emotion.)

JOEY: (Sings) You're never alone/never alone. I'll encourage you/ you're never alone. I'll protect you/you're never alone. I love you/ you're never alone. I'm here for you/I'm here for you. You're never alone/never alone You're never-ever-alone.

(Joey stops singing.)

JOEY: I'm here for you.

(Old Louey still stares into deep space. Joey wipes the tears from his eyes.)

JOEY: I hope you hear me, Pop. I really hope you do. I love you, Pop. I always will. I'm here for you.

(Joey slowly turns away from his father. Old Louey slowly grabs Joey's hand. Joey turns back to see his father smiling at him with a large happy grin. Old Louey stands and is eye to eye with his son. Joey's joy is extraordinary.)

JOEY: (Overwhelming joy) I knew you could hear me. I knew it.

(Joey hugs his father.)

JOEY: You're back, Pop. You're back!

(Joey and Old Louey break from the hug.)

JOEY: You're back. Miracles do happen, Pop.

(Old Louey smiles on. Then he begins to sing.)

Old Louey: (Sings) I'm here for you/you're never alone. I'm here for you/you're never alone.

JOEY: You sing like you used to, Pop.

Old Louey: (Sings on) I love you/you're never alone.

(Old Louey starts to walk away from Joey.)

Old Louey: You're never alone/never alone. I'm here for you/you're never alone.

(Old Louey starts to exit stage left. Joey becomes confused.)

JOEY: Where you going, Pop?

Old Louey: (Singing) You're-never-ever-alone.

(Old Louey exits stage left completely.)

JOEY: Come back, Pop! Don't leave me again! Come back!

(Joey screams out for his father.)

JOEY: Come back, Pop! I'm here for you now!!! I'm here now!! I'm sorry, Pop! I'm sorry!

(Joey yells out in desperation.)

JOEY: I'm here for you!!!

(A loud voice is heard in the background.)

Male Voice: What the hell is going on in there, Romero? You talking to yourself?

(Joey is silent in his helpless state.)

Male Voice: Keep it down! You'll wake up the whole damn block!

(Joey remains silent as reality sets in.)

Male Voice: Do you understand me, Romero? Huh?

JOEY: I understand, officer. I understand.

(Silence. Joey stands there in total despair, a broken man, lost in regret. He lowers his head. His arms drop to his side.)

(The lights darken on the stage. Joey backs away in the darkness.)

(Silence.)

The End.

Fielding Dawson Prize, Drama

King of Infinite Space
CHRIS DANKOVICH

[ACT III, Scene II]

JOHN sits in small, armless chair in sparse holding room. JOHN stands up, pacing. ELIJAH GRAY watches and listens.

JOHN: So I sit here, lay here, stand here, walk around in circles... hour after hour, day after day until days and hours and months and years mean nothing to me. I feel at home with the things in this world that do not move. I imagine myself immovable. I am a mountain, immovable, majestic, powerful... but the truth is, the hills and valleys and stones and earth are none of that. They are not powerful. Treacherous? Yes. Dangerous? Yes. But powerful? No. Power comes from influence over life, over movement, which the immovable do not do except with fear and shadows to drive those things away from them.
As a young child, I hiked through the mountains. I found pottery from old civilizations smashed on the ground, bones of men and animals strewn about, some like new, some like stone. But there

was no difference. It was in that moment that I felt I discovered a secret, a horrible secret of the universe, one that if revealed, it would destroy... one that if let out, it would infect and kill. As I stood there, looking at the eternal, the only thing that would always be was nothing. All the striving and all the movement and all the toil adds up to nothing in the end. Our achievements will be forgotten. Our monuments will fall. Our lives will have no more impact on the world than a single one of those stones or bones. Movement is power, but power is nothing. We are nothing in the end.

ELIJAH: We are nothing except when we are alive, but then we die. Were we always nothing if we are nothing in the end?

JOHN: I have seen the best of men cut down while the vilest keep running forward. I have seen innocent women and children cast aside and around like nothing. So what is virtue, what is good, what is valued when everything can merely be cast away? When even the best is destroyed one day?

ELIJAH: So because things can be cast aside, you become one who does the casting. And if nothing exists, then you choose to side with nothing?

JOHN: I choose the side of what is real! I choose to know the truth and not waste my time, any more than it is already wasted in the state of being. To give my heart and soul to that which is nothing... to value and hold dear that which is but a spectre in the fog on a moonless cloudy night... that is what I become.

ELIJAH: You become nothing when you accept what you say is nothing? As opposed to what you are now, a criminal of the world, a warmonger, a destroyer...

JOHN: What I am is... real. What I am is... truth. What I am is purely... man. And in my nature, I am a god.

ELIJAH: What about God?

JOHN: A deceiver! A chess-player with us as the pawns. He creates for us a world where the space between holes are infinitely greater than the whole. He is the fire, and our world nothing but moving patterns of smoke and clouds, shapes meaning nothing the moment after they appear, never to appear again.

ELIJAH: What about love?

JOHN:What about it?

ELIJAH: Does love mean nothing?

JOHN: Love is... love...

JOHN looks nervously around. Ponders.

ELIJAH: Because only someone who has never loved or has lost love so completely could ever say it was nothing.

(continued...)

One of the most important things to know about the imprisoned writer experience is the difficult balance we have to strike in separating our grievances and our gripes from our Art. If it is pure grievance disguised as Art, then, I believe, it is unlikely to be truly absorbed or appreciated by the reader. And our everyday lives are overwhelmed with grievance—not just the superficial grievances that are a consequence of imprisonment itself, but the earnest human rights grievances that are the catalyst for reform and revolution. Just within the past week, I've personally experienced a week-long lockdown which was initiated with a unit shakedown (rooms tossed asunder) by 70+ rookie guards, as over 260 inmates stood idle, crammed onto a small, muddy rec. field for four hours. How do I make such an experience relatable to a middle class father of three from the financial district of New York or to a 60-year old retiree from a low-crime cul-de-sac of Connecticut? That is the balance. To go beyond the individual agonies to tap into the collective humanity that we all can identify with.

—Jevon Jackson
2019 First Place Prize in Poetry,
PEN America Prison Writing Awards

2019 PEN AMERICA
PRISON WRITING AWARDS
HONORABLE MENTION

Honorable Mention, Fiction

Tetris
JAMES PHILIP BEAVERS

"Why wont this music stop!?"

Kyle sat on his mat on the concrete slab of a bunk. His hands were propped on the sides of his head as he stared up at the fluorescent lights burning two long lines into his vision. He had been in the hole for two weeks and still had two more to go. His cell was empty, except for his cup, spoon, soap, clothes and a Bible. Luckily, he had sneaked a pack of playing cards in his waistband. But one tires of Solitaire, and he couldn't sleep anymore. All he saw were the two lines. The music was returning. He was going mad. This was the Hole.

They had put him in the Hole because of a fight. He had tangoed with this Mexican over words. He broke the other guy's nose and had a good scrap. However, he got a concussion when his shorter opponent rushed him and pushed his head into the metal top bunk of the cell, crossing his vision. After the guards had come in and separated them in different holding cells, he called for help with a skull-splitting headache. No help came. Days later the administration pulled each of them out to a disciplinary court; both were sentenced to thirty days in the hole.

The officer led Kyle to his cell down a long hallway; each cell was separated by at least five feet on stacked concrete blocks. Like a little one room apartment: bed, table, toilet and shower.

He set up his routine: Shower, exercise, shower, sleep, and read. The only way he could measure the days and nights was by the light playing across the walls from the window at the end of the hall. If you were caught talking, you weren't fed that day.

The second week came and went much the same but there was something new in his tiny world. The walls began to close in on him. From the time he woke to the time he fell asleep, the music from the game Tetris played. The circular, 8-bit music drilled into his mind.

By the fourth week he had been reduced to a mute mess. He had continued to eat his meals and keep up his personal cleanliness but it was all done as a habit. He was afraid to think; if he did the music would return.

Officer Tagwell stepped up to the cell, looking at Kyle. "Marshall, Kyle. You're done in the Hole."

The guard led him out and down the hallway to the elevator. Kyle moved into his new cell. He wasn't there more than an hour before the chaplain called him to the visitation booth.

"Your aunt called us to check on you. Are you okay?"

"I was in the Hole," Kyle replied flatly. "My father is dead, isn't he?"

"Yes, son."

Kyle set the phone receiver down like it was an egg, afraid to have anything else in his life break. He shook his head and thought back to the letter from his father. The true pain came from watching his father's handwriting slowly deteriorate through the cancer, the once-flowing script turning into an illegible mess.

Kyle went to the telephone to call Mary. Mary really wasn't his aunt, but a lady who worked for a lawyer's office that he knew. She was as close to family as possible in this situation. He heard the recognizable click of the recorder as she answered the phone.

"Hey, Mary, the chaplain just called me out to talk to me. How did it all happen?"

"He was released on a bond to a hospice. He died that night. The fifth of last month."

Today was the first. A whole month later.

"Mary . . . get me some help, please."

Hours later Kyle was escorted to the psychiatric wing of the jail. Here he had a bunk and toilet, nothing else. They took his sheets and clothes so he couldn't hang himself. He ate with a styrofoam cup and wasn't allowed to shower for three days. Mary had called the jail and told the officers in charge that she was worried for his safety.

Kyle laid there on his bunk, naked, listening to the screams and pounding of the other patients on the wing. Kyle hummed the music aloud, rocking his knees back and forth. He watched the yellow tiles on the wall move down and stack together to make lines. Building around a hole he would never crawl out from.

Please visit the contest archives at pen.org/prison-writing for the full piece.

Honorable Mention, Fiction

Two Birds, One Stone
BRENDAN RAO

Brady's toes squirm in the sand. His eyes stare downward at the shifting grains, barely noticing the warmth seeping into his feet. What he was most aware of, yet least willing to look at, was the endless expanse of water just beyond his vision. Never in his life had he been confronted by a body of water he couldn't see the opposite bank of. Now, if he raised his head, he'd first see waves leaping nearly as high as he stood, and beyond that—water, just endless water for as far as he could see. His mom, in her floral swimsuit, had tried to lead him by his hand down the gentle slope to the water but the advancing and retreating water reminded him too much of a cat's paw extending to capture a mouse. Many times he'd watched the family tom catch and release a mouse with a bored indolence, and the rhythm of the water was too similar to Kitty's predatory certitude. He knew what Kitty did when the mouse stopped being entertaining, and in the face of the ocean, he didn't doubt it would be bored with him on the instant. The alien scent of the saltwater mixing with the candy-sweet smell of the sunscreen his mother slathered on his face and back, the sound of the gulls crying and the people yelling and splashing in the crashing surf, all combining was just too much. His stomach heaves then clenches.

As we rise through conflicting air currents, our wings jitter as we shift into the formation we'd trained for. The mission profile allowed for a little leeway, but for this, my first mission, I have but one goal: my first kill. We didn't have sophisticated targeting systems— no radar-guided or heat-seeking anything. Just timing and gravity. You learn your airframe, you learn to read the currents of the wind and its resistances. You learn acceleration and deceleration and momentum. And you practice, practice, practice. Hitting a stationary target is now second nature. I can release a payload and be maneuvering away long before the target is struck, but until today, I've never fired at a living, breathing, moving target.

Our flight path has taken us over territory I know well. Far below us, the sea meets the sand. Happy, frolicking families pepper the beach. I dip a wing and roll, nose down scanning the sand for a likely target.

They say you never forget your first.

Brady's mom has been watching him and knows, as only a mother does, exactly what Brady needs: a distraction. She reaches into their red plastic cooler and pulls out something wrapped in white paper. "Hey Brady," she calls "you want a popsicle? I've got a chocolate one here." She waves the package at Brady enticingly. "Use both hands, Honey," she says as his tiny fingers wrap around the wooden stick. As he takes his first nibble of the frosty sweetness, his mom puts her hands on his shoulders and turns him towards the water. With all of Brady's attention focused on the icy, creamy texture of his popsicle, he takes no notice of how close his mother has steered him towards the foaming breakers. His mother steps back a few paces and watches to be certain Brady isn't panicking. Seeing his absorption, she continues to the shade of their giant umbrella. She thinks she's making progress in acclimating Brady, her baby boy, into enjoying the ocean. She has only led a lamb to slaughter.

Is this fate? Is it favor from the gods? There, almost directly below me, in my flight path, a target all alone, oblivious to the world around him. This is it. I have my first target. With a few minor adjustments I'm diving, accelerating. My vision has tunnelled to see only a small boy savoring a snack-on-a-stick. Everything is happening by muscle memory alone. Three, two, one… I release a primal scream.

Brady looks up and his face becomes a mask of horror. Reflexively, he gasps, his mouth gaping wide, sucking in a breath to power a scream.

My eyes bulge. The blood in my veins sings. At this point, missing is an impossibility. If anyone saw my face, they'd think the velocity of my dive formed a grim rictus, but if they looked closer, they'd understand it was really a feral grin. This would be more than just a simple hit and run. This would be that hallowed, vaunted Double Kill. Time-on-target: Zero.

Please visit the contest archives at pen.org/prison-writing for the full piece.

Honorable Mention, Fiction

Rogers Park: Area 52
ANTONIO BOWIE-RIVERA

The landing happened about two years before my release date but Rogers Park had become a Martian landscape for me long before. When you're on the inside, the outside world fades away. If you come from a large city, like I do, there is this feeling that you're on another planet when you make it out to where most prisons are. You aren't accustomed to the wide open spaces and lack of noise.

I'd walk around the yard and try to peer past the fences and take in the humble serenity and natural beauty that surrounded the hell hole I was in. Even the rolling farmland that sat right outside the barbed wire double gates seemed like it was a million miles away. Your whole life is the few feet of space the state gives you, and you become so preoccupied with making sure no one takes it away from you or maintaining what semblance of dignity you can manage after the strip searches, the racial bashing from guards and other inmates, the "food" you wouldn't feed to a rat you were trying to kill, that you forget about the world as much as it's forgotten about you.

And believe me it has.

You fantasize about getting out; you walk through your old hood in your daydreams but when you actually get there it's foreign, like putting your right foot in the left boot. There's a Starbucks where the corner store used to be and instead of little old Hispanic ladies and their seventeen grandkids running around, you see these lily-white hipster kids walking three-legged shelter dogs. You go back to the corner bar down from your house for dollar beers but instead you find a gastro-pub where everything is bacon flavored for some reason and your favorite bartender, Mickey, has been replaced with some rude punk chick with half her head shaved.

You just wanted to come home: to the corner under the streetlight where you had your first kiss, or the alley you learned to ride your bike in, but isn't anymore. You want to move everything back to its place like so much old furniture, but you can't.

And, you want the UFO's off the beach your mom took you to every weekend, but there they are, twelve of them, 200 feet tall, perfectly cylindrical, two feet in diameter with a glimmering silver finish, all arranged in a circle nearly 100 feet across.

I left a world where nothing is soft and pain is the natural state of things, a meat grinder whose crank is the law, and whose gnashing teeth are a product of a society that wants to hide the scars of its face from a mirror it cannot look away from.

I came home to a world of self-driving cars and an idiot game show host who had somehow become president. I came home and you couldn't say the word "fag" anymore and parents didn't let their kids play outside. I came home and augmented reality was king, whatever the fuck that was. Who'd have thought that the strangest thing about coming home from prison wouldn't be the goddamned aliens parked on the beach down the block?

My halfway house was a couple blocks away from Loyola Beach: ground zero or area: 52 as it came to be called. I couldn't get a good night's sleep on account of the choppers and jets that were constantly coming and going. It was bright as hell too, like a night game at Wrigley, only it was every night. And the people! Oh my god the people...

"It's a sign from God!"

"They've come to save us!"

"Take us with you!"

I couldn't think of anything worth saving less than the human race. If they were here to do anything, I hoped it was to blow this planet to smithereens.

I gazed at the pillars for a long time. I could kind of feel them, like there was a low hum coming from inside of me, but I knew it was the pillars somehow. Not a physical pull but something else, like watching a baby take its first steps. It just kind of happens like it was always going to happen. I remember lighting my square but not taking a single drag. When the heat of the red-hot cherry got near my fingers, I flicked the butt over the banister and rubbed the burnt spot on my hand. When I looked up again at the pillars, the pull and the hum were gone.

I can't say exactly when I got it in my head but I needed something out of those silver sticks or maybe they needed something out of me. I wasn't sure I could live a full and complete life, a life worth living at all, without getting my hands on one.

I'd get off the train and take the long way home, the way that meant walking past the sandbags on Sheridan Road. The way with triple gates with barbed wire, armed National Guardsman every ten feet, and high-tech guard towers manned by sharp shooters. I was used to the towers and men with guns willing to put a bullet in you for looking at them wrong. I knew that feeling well: far from home in a place where everyone is suspicious of you and no way to get out. Being watched constantly and having guns trained on you everywhere you go.

I started to feel connected to these things. I felt like they understood me, like they knew where I'd been and the things I'd gone through like no one else ever would or could...

Please visit the contest archives at pen.org/prison-writing for the full piece.

Honorable Mention, Memoir

Under the Bridge
CHRISTIANA JUSTICE

Not too many things are difficult to deal with when you're high as a kite, soaring above the crowds of people on the streets of DC. It's no New York, but that suits me just fine. You can breathe a little better here in Chocolate City. I'm floating, wrapped in the warmest blanket you can only create with water and a needle. The only thread you need is your tie-off, and the contents of the blanket fit into a spoon. Or a bottle cap. Or even a tin can if you're in a tight spot. Any junkie will be very resourceful when it comes to the love of their life. But even this warm blanket can't keep the chill of a rainy night on the streets away forever.

See, when it rains in the city, all the best stoops are snapped up by the seasoned people on the streets—those who have been homeless the longest. I wonder if it's because they feel the change in the air, so they know to find shelter, or if there's some kind of underground communication by the street veterans when one of them catches the weather on a tv or radio. Either way, they've learned how to avoid what I'm going through now. The rest of us out here, fresh to the streets, new and uncertain, plus a scattering of hard-core alcoholics have to take the next best option.

Looking around in the eery light, I'm surprised half of these people made it to cover. They might as well be sitting in the downpour for how inebriated they are; I'm not sure they would even notice the rain. I suppose since they've been doing this so long, that even in their incoherent state, they are creatures of habit. Though their minds may be gone, drowning in a bottle, their bodies know to scurry to the nearest bridge, to make it just marginally easier to get their next fix tomorrow. Begging for change is difficult if you're extra rank from not bathing because your clothes are already damp. It becomes a losing battle. I should know.

It's dark under here, our only light a flickering street lamp down the way, but my eyes have adjusted to it. I am eternally grateful that I have two blankets. One of itchy wool, the other of that crunchy, dark brown heroin. The heroin makes me less afraid of the night creatures I am surrounded by, and almost entirely accepting of the fact I'm sleeping under a bridge tonight. It used to smell bad under here but I've gotten so accustomed to it I don't notice all the bodies and their smells or even my own.

I'm far away from a quiet, suburban home with a white picket fence. I threw it all out the window just for one more fix, the price I paid for my true love, heroin. I traded my life and my soul to the devil, injecting him straight into my now non-existent veins. Last night I had to pay a fellow bum a ten-piece of crack to hit me in my jugular, because I can't go in my hands any more, and the pain of shooting up in my feet when I'm dopesick is simply too much to bear.

One of my blankets is fading away, and the damp chill of reality is creeping up too fast for comfort, and I'm alone.

Please visit the contest archives at pen.org/prison-writing for the full piece.

Honorable Mention, Memoir

Confessions of a Penitentiary Death Dealer

KYLE HEDQUIST

The crumpled penitentiary newsletter lay in my makeshift garbage can; like most weeks the news meant little to me. I was twenty-one years old and the last thing I was interested in was this, the last article I read before tossing the newspaper in my trash.

The article read like a "Help Wanted" sign. The exciting and new opportunity being offered was a program called Hospice, a program I had never heard about, that was being established in the prison infirmary, a place I had never been. Volunteers were needed to take care of a bunch of old men dying in the infirmary (most of them probably sex-offenders). Just like I thought, another worthless article.

I was a convicted murderer, why would I want to care for strangers dying in a prison infirmary? At the same time, my grandfather slowly dying from Parkinson's disease, and I felt helpless behind the 25-foot concrete walls. Two weeks later, I received notice of an interview.

The room was coated in the multiple layers of dingy white paint only seen in prison. The floors were the color of coldness and worn from decades of scrubbing and machine-wheel wear. Three prison staffers sat behind a table questioning my interest and motivation for volunteering for this new program. At twenty-two years old, I was the youngest applicant. I had very little interest and I didn't know what had motivated me to apply. Nevertheless, I found myself attending a twelve-week community-led training course.

We soon had three "clients". The dying prisoner had to sign up to participate in Hospice. I quickly found myself sitting with a terminally ill man, who, otherwise, was much like myself. We were both confused and afraid. I didn't know of what, but I had never met death. Despite being in prison for murder, I was uncomfortable with the idea of being with someone as they died. Sometimes all I could do was sit and listen, I didn't like that I wanted to "do" something. But I sat and listened to shallow labored breathing, and stared at cold clammy hands laying atop sheets that needed changing several times a day. I had never changed an adult diaper before, but early on in my training I had made up my mind that no client of mine would sit in his own feces and urine.

From my clients, I learned a lot about how the body prepares to leave this Earth. Death, I would learn, comes on its own terms and in its own time. Death is a heavy damp fog that leaves every room bitterly cold. Its smell would permeate my clothing and my hands. I could taste death on my lips, my eyes would burn when I left the room and entered the bright sunlight and filled my lungs with fresh air. Some clients left quietly almost with a sense of peace others left this world violently, full of pain and fear. Death came for all of them, it took them and waits for each of us. The Hispanic population had a nickname for us, Death Dealers; they revered death and saw us as warriors in the battle between Death and Life. I didn't feel like I was winning any battles. I sat for years with dozens of dying men, I sacrificed my free time, spent hours listening to their stories, their regrets and yes even their confessions of brutal crimes: murder, rape, child molestation. They were all liars and thieves. The more I heard, the dirtier I felt. I became angry and thought that maybe this way some cruel cosmic justice.

Was this Death's final punishment for criminals? Would this be my punishment for my crime? I couldn't have known all those years ago that death would bring my humanity back. So I sat, I listened, their teary-eyed regurgitation of their crimes burned my ears they left a bitter taste in my mouth as I consumed the confessions. Their pain would burrow itself into my flesh, my heart weighed heavy, at times I was emotionally drained and physically exhausted as I carried their pain. Was this my punishment for murdering someone? I strove to feel their regrets; I wrapped their sorrows around my shivering body like a worn-out hospital blanket. I couldn't understand, but somehow just being with them and listening lightened their burden before death stepped in to take them. There were times that I witnessed death's arrival. But I knew he was always near, counting the breaths as I did hour by hour. Sometimes I didn't want him to come; I cried in my cell not wanting my relationship to end, "not yet," I would whisper.

My grandfather died and I didn't hold his hand. I didn't change his bedding. I did not have the privilege of listening to his story—did he have regrets, did he have confessions to make? I wasn't there when death came for him. I didn't plead with death to wait. I've questioned my motives, my purpose, and my role in prison. Murder brought me to this place, but it was dealing with death that brought me back to life. I will spend the rest of my life in prison for the crimes I committed. But you will find me sitting, listening, and waiting to meet Death in the cold infirmary of the State Penitentiary.

Honorable Mention, Memoir

Murderers' Ball
MICHAEL WILLIE

The Murderers' Ball is what we call the annual fall Lifer's Club banquet. It's mostly said in jest and among ourselves, Lifers that is. It's dark humor shared by those of us who are in for life because we took a life.

When I first came down, I didn't know anybody, and I didn't have anything. I refused to ask for help from my friends and family. I wanted them to consider me dead and carry on with their lives. This was the same logic I used in the Death Penalty Phase of my trial: I refused to subject most of my friends and family by having them take the stand on my behalf. I wouldn't even let my mother beg for her own sons' life. That's what shame and guilt does to a man. And breaking all ties with the past, well that's what Life Without Parole (LWOP) does to a man. At the time I thought I was doing them a favor and myself one as well.

Within the first couple weeks or so after I arrived here at the Penitentiary, two scruffy, long haired, tattooed individuals coming up to my cell, called me by name and handed me a good-sized brown paper bag of miscellaneous hygiene and other canteen items including coffee, tobacco, toothpaste, envelopes, cups, candy, sugar, creamer, razors... etc through the bars of my cell. I remember pushing it back through to them, telling them that I didn't want it, couldn't afford it and wasn't looking for any favors. One of the first things you learn, from day one in county jail, is to not go into debt.

"No, no, no," the first guy said, "it isn't like that. This is a gift to you from the Lifer's Club. We don't want anything in return. We are just reaching out to welcome you and to let you know that you are not alone in here. Lifers look out for Lifers."

"You're a Lifer and you don't need to be living like this," he continued, motioning with a sweep of his arm at my cellie and me in our small two-man cell that was originally made for single occupancy. It was a very dank and cramped quarters for even one person.

"We'll get you a single cell," he said.

Within a week I was moving into a single cell and away from that cellie whose name I can no longer remember. I don't remember the names of the two Lifers from that morning either, I don't even remember thanking them properly. But I do remember how deeply that little encounter affected my early incarceration.

When I stumbled into joining the Lifer's club I honestly went for the free soda that they offered.

"Free soda? You're shitting me," I said.

"Yep, no strings attached, just show up to a meeting," my Lifer friend said.

I had never been one for attending meetings and obligating myself for more responsibility. Actually, I had made a career at avoiding such things. But at the time it had probably been a couple of years since I had tasted a soda, so that is how I first joined a club.

At that first meeting I also remember looking around seeing the faces of guys I didn't know, and I didn't want to know. I figured that I didn't have anything in common with these guys except for a body. You look into these faces and think to yourself how could this be the face of someone who killed somebody, or into the next face and tell yourself, yes, now that is a face of a murderer.

Then when you get back to your cell, and you look into the mirror at your still young face and see nothing of a murderer in it. You raise your chin and turn your profile and then you see it, the self-inflicted wound with its still fresh pink scar from trying to take your own life after taking hers.

After a year or so the taste of soda wore thin. I didn't know what the ins and outs of the club were and honestly didn't take the time to find out. My mind wasn't to the point of being able to think of others and their concerns, I was still filled with hate and discontent, mostly at myself, and I was still just trying to wrap my head around the reality of "Life Without Parole." Playing softball and hiding from my past behind these big grey walls was my new routine. At one point I avoided looking over the walls for nearly 7 years. Somehow or another I had let a couple of meetings slip by without my attending, and if you miss two consecutive meetings you are no longer considered to be a member in good standings and membership is terminated.

It would take me more than a decade to come back to the Lifer's Club and give it another chance. I had beaten my LWOP down to Life w/30, which in itself motivated me. There was a new power shift in the executive body, which carried a sense of a new direction for the club. With all this new energy it felt like the timing was right to rejoin the club. It's common knowledge here in the Penitentiary that the Lifer's Club always treats its membership the best and really steps it up for the banquets. After getting a taste of them, these banquets were a top priority for me now.

I had a pretty good run at the Lifer's Club that second time and was a member in good standing for several years, but still had only begun to get my feet wet learning about all the club's programs and activities. Still these meeting were more of a social gathering for me. I had some friends, whom I didn't see as often as I would have liked. It was good to reconnect with them at the meetings. I found it enjoyable to donate my time, materials and energy from the hobby shop to help support our program and volunteers, but the important part was that I was donating something to someone beside myself.

Around this same time my mind became occupied with the Parole Board and everything that entails. The closer I got to my 20 year mark and my first parole hearing the more I started to worry about doing things that would impress the parole board. Only being allowed to join three clubs, I chose to drop Lifer's and join AA/NA, which seemed to be the only programming recognized by the Parole Board. I've since found that all volunteer work is from the heart and not meant for anything else but for the good of the cause itself. But back then, I wasn't quite there yet and was still mostly concerned about my own wants and needs and jumping through the hoops for the Parole Board. Another decade or so would pass by before I found myself joining the club now for my third time.

Maybe it has just taken this long to understand the way things work. Rejection and hearing NO doesn't affect me as it once did in my youth. When you volunteer your time for a club and start getting into the nuts and bolts of it all, you learn that it's not uncommon to be working on a worthy and beneficial project only to be shot down at the last moment. Chain of command works that way. I remember a mentor's word of advice to me at the time of starting my volunteer work.

"Keep asking. They can't say no forever because our forever will be way past their forever. Their forever is retirement."

Next month we will have our first of two Murderers' Balls. Our club is so big that we are granted two. Our visiting room that acts as a dining hall for these banquets has a capacity for only 85 prisoners and their guests. Members are allowed to bring in a guest from their visiting list. Our members who have guests look forward to spending this time sharing a meal with a loved one. Food from the outside is the big draw for the bachelors (those without a guest) attending the Ball. Good food is damn near everything to prisoners. Some years we have Chinese food. Some years we have BBQ Ribs and Chicken. Last year we had "build your own" Hamburgers and Hotdogs, like a picnic. But this year's ball might top them all with Beef Brisket and Chicken. And we always have plenty of ice cream to go around. We wish that everyone incarcerated could experience a banquet with good food, good atmosphere, good conversation and most importantly, less noise and congestion than chow hall dinners. Community connections and keeping these connections is so important for successful reentry. The real shame is that we don't have more ways to have these connections with family, friends and loved ones throughout the year.

A previous administration rescinded the Lifer's Club privilege of giving away gift packs to the newly arrived Lifer because it violated a code of conduct rule that states, "An inmate cannot give, trade, borrow or steal property from another inmate." But we keep trying to reinstate it, us old school Lifers who remember the benefits of such a program.

But we do have the Murderers' Ball. And at the banquet are people in our community who are trying to make a difference. Some of them may not even know it yet, like I didn't. They'll have to go through a "gestation" period like I did, and like the generations of Lifers before me did.

Please visit the contest archives at pen.org/prison-writing for the full piece.

Parole Reform
DANIEL PIRKEL

Parole boards have the arduous responsibility of deciding when, if ever, convicted felons are returned to society. The problem is that no one but God can do this with 100% accuracy. Therefore, they sometimes release dangerous criminals, and in other cases, they allow rehabilitated, productive individuals to rot in prison. Deciphering the difference between these types of individuals is tricky for many reasons. While parole boards may spend a fair amount of time combing through prisoner files and personally interviewing each potential parolee, manipulative people sometimes say and do all of the right things to leave interviewers with a favorable impression. In contrast, many decent human beings interview poorly, especially when they are being judged for the worst behavior of their lives (not a very enjoyable experience). Aside from lacking charisma, some people contradict the Presentence Investigation Report (PSI) because they are actually innocent of the crimes that they were convicted of, but guilty of lesser crimes. Parole boards consider all such deviations as attempts by unrepentant criminals to avoid taking responsibility and diminish their roles in the crime(s). The problem with this philosophy is that prosecutors often overcharge people, and then coerce them into taking unfair pleas by threatening to either give them more time or to charge family member with more crimes. In addition, there is clear evidence that many incarcerated people are actually innocent.

According to the Innocence Project, 319 people have been exonerated using DNA evidence since 1989.1 Furthermore, Scheck, Neufeld, and Dwyer (2001) found that 88 of the 6,000 people on death row between 1976 and 2001 were wrongly convicted, while only 664 of the 6,000 were executed. With our faulty appellate court system, this is likely only a very small fraction of those who are unjustly imprisoned.

Perhaps the most significant critique that can be made about parole board decisions is their reliance on political influence instead of objective statistical risk assessments. For example, nonviolent offenders are the most likely to be paroled, but the most likely to reoffend. In contrast, violent offenders are the least likely to reoffend, but the least likely to be paroled. According to an article called, "Paroling people who committed serious crimes; What is the actual risk?,"4 only 204 out of the 6,673 (3.1%) sex offenders released from 1986-1999 committed another sex offense. An even lower reoffense rate applied to those who had been convicted of homicide. These numbers stand in drastic contrast to the recidivism rates among all convicted felons (roughly 67%). This disparity occurs partly because of public perception. Shows like CSI and America's Most Wanted have sensationalized heinous crimes, making the majority of the public believe that violent offenders are the most likely to repeat their criminal behavior. Even though parole boards know better, it is still riskier for them to parole someone with such a past because of the potential for political backlash. If a prior drug offender commits a new crime, it will barely make a footnote in a newspaper (unless it is a very serious crime).

However, if a sex offender reoffends, the story could wind up on Fox News. Since Parole Board members are appointed by the governor (in Michigan), it takes nothing to fire them. Conversely, there is almost no risk for the parole board to arbitrarily flop someone. Prisoners cannot appeal these decisions, and suing them in federal court is nearly impossible.

So how do we fix this broken system? Many advocates argue that providing clear parole guidelines will make the parole process fairer. Allegedly, this limits the parole board's discretion, preventing it from denying a potential parolee unless he or she fails to meet certain criteria, like failing to have a parole plan. However, altering guidelines is a meaningless tactic if parole boards cannot be held accountable for abusing their discretion in carrying out those guidelines. Therefore, prisoners must have a mode in which they can challenge the state's actions in parole decisions. Any system that cannot be held accountable is an unjust system.

Some might argue that incarcerated people deserve to be cheated, as they committed grievous crimes against innocent people. This seems to be a good point until we consider the consequences of such a position. First, cheating people accused of crimes increases the chances that innocent ones will become "collateral damage." Second, long term incarceration has been proven to be detrimental to people's mental health. Third, empirical evidence indicates that people are more likely to comply and cooperate with authorities when they appear legitimate (i.e. just), not through the fear of potential repercussions. Since our government's perceived legitimacy directly relates to how people are treated by police officers and the courts, holding authorities accountable is just as big of a security issue as placing wrongdoers behind bars. How we treat criminal defendants is especially important when we consider that 95% of prisoners eventually return to society. The question is, how many will come home broken and worse off than when they were incarcerated? How can we expect people to magically become rehabilitated by placing them in terrible conditions for long periods of time? More often than not, they become embittered, hollow, and lose respect for those in authority because of the lack of procedural justice they have experienced.

Regardless of how we cut it, the system needs a serious overhaul. Our government is notorious for repeating the same "mistakes" over and over, the very definition of insanity. So what can the average citizen do to change things? First, we must learn about what type of issues can make a significant, positive difference. We need to know enough that we will not be tricked by ambiguous affirmations of favoring "criminal justice reform" from politicians that only want our vote. There are organizations like the Coalition for Justice Voters (CJV) that have done the research on political candidates, giving each a different grade based on how they have voted or answered questions in the past. Second, we must make it clear to those in authority that we care about criminal justice issues. Write letters, emails, call their office, or offer to take them out for lunch. If officials do not want to pass legislation that can dramatically affect the prison system, e.g. reinstituting good time, then we must sign petitions to get the issue placed on the ballot. We can make a difference regardless of who is in Lansing or Washington. We just need the desire and knowledge to do something about it.

Please visit the contest archives at pen.org/prison-writing for the full piece.

Illustration by Lafayette Wa

Triple Sessions
KEVIN D. SAWYER

"You get water when we tell you to," the coach would say. That almost always meant after practice. I don't recall any player ever walking away from the practice field to get a drink of water. That was unheard of, and there was never a thermos on the field. We learned quickly to fill up on water before practice and to replenish our bodies afterward. Practice would end with wind sprints. We would run twenty forty-yard dashes. "Hands down, on the line," the coach would shout. "Set. At the sound of the whistle go." The whistle controlled a lot of our movement. It told us when to start or stop something. If one of my teammates jogged across the line the coach wouldn't count that sprint so we'd have to repeat it until twenty acceptable sprints were completed. "That one didn't count. Number fifty-four wasn't running," the coach would say. Some days we'd run about twenty-three forty-yard dashes—an additional one hundred and twenty yards. That's the length of a football field and both end zones. The twenty forties equaled half mile by itself.

"Get down and put your asses on the chalk line," was the coaches next demand after our sprints were done. We were out of breath as he'd say, "Hands on your cage. Fifty sit-ups. At the sound of the whistle pull yourselves up and go back down." And just like the wind sprints, one of my teammates would invariably not sit up at the sound of the whistle. "That one didn't count," the coach would say. He let us know that we were going to suffer as a team, lose as a team, and win as a team. "If one man doesn't pull his weight during a game, we all lose. Do it over."

"Good practice, men," the coach would tell us with a few more words of encouragement. "See you at five o'clock sharp." It wasn't a reminder, but more of an admonishment. "Four O'clock chalk talk for receivers." That meant we had to report to our school's orange and black painted, must-filled weight room adjacent the locker room and showers an hour before the next practice started. We were immune to the smell of the boys locker room because we were boys. We were inoculated with the vaccination to protect our noses in junior high. By the time we entered high school our combined odors in the gym had become a normal part of school. Only the girls noticed the stench of the boys locker room when they passed by the open door, and they'd often tell us about it, as if boys cared.

"Some of you guys may think we're too hard on you, but one day you'll thank us," the coach once said. "A lot of our athletes graduate and go to the military. Some have told us that they wouldn't have made it through basic training if it had not been for their experience playing high school football." I've always viewed every high school football team as America's standing military. All prep sports, but especially football prepare young men for the military and beyond.

Please visit the contest archives at pen.org/prison-writing for the full piece.

Lexie's Books

DANIEL WHITLOW

Diagnosed with leukemia at eleven, and confined to a wheelchair, Lexie was an avid reader. We became close friends in the third grade, and spent much of our time together, before her diagnosis and after, discussing poetry, and what inspired us to take our next step. Her favorite poet was Edna St. Vincent-Millay and she would read and reread her works to me, never losing her connection with eternal wonder and sublime joy, even after her diseased reality laid its profane mark on her delicate body—the type of bliss reserved for the truly alive. In those moments, inundated by waters of infinite inspiration, she was immortal; she was invincible and could not be beaten. In those moments, she was more alive than I was.

After a few years of terrifying struggle, at the tender age of fourteen, she succumbed to her sickness. In her will, she graciously blessed me with her poetry collection, an exhaustive, ten-book anthology of American authors I had not seen before. Each book of the anthology was filled with Lexie's notes, observations and feelings she openly shared with the pages. I wept at the sight of her thoughts, as if she was speaking to me from the grave. A ponderous mass of sorrow crushed me and I ran from it like a coward, unable to bear its weight. I invented excuses to avoid confronting the absence I felt in my heart and life. I came up with ways to evade immersing myself in the consecrating wells of her most intimate interpretations, because if I did, she would truly be gone and nothing frightened me more. I would say things like, "I'm too busy" and "the books will be there tomorrow"—they were, but I never was. For many years, I could not understand why the hurt did not go away. It took my grandpa almost breaking his neck to show me why.

One fine Sunday morning, my mother proudly declared, "Today, we're cleaning out the attic." I cringed. The attic smelled awful. Wet, rotting, squirming unpleasantness seeped out of every flimsy-looking floorboard and ominous inch of pink panther insulation. You know when you smell something so terrible, so putrid you can taste it? "Oh geez," my papa said. "That's not a good smell." He began making his way forward pinching his nostrils closed, colorfully elaborating on how "not good" the smell was when his foot caught the corner of a box, and he tripped, falling like a redwood. "Aw, crap!" Fortunately, before he crashed, he was able to realign himself and fall onto a pile of old blankets, billowing dust clouds exploding in response. Unfortunately, the old blankets were home to the stench, now blanketing us with spore-like foulness.

After I finished laughing—and coughing—and made sure he was okay, I set upon the cardboard culprit. As I opened the box flaps, my breath caught in my chest, sweat prickling across my brow; the sight of familiar spines staring back at me with reproach, brushed with a layer of time and neglect, caused my stomach to feel light and loose in my guts. It had only been a few years since Lexie died but my avoidance was constant. Guilt, and shame, climbed up my throat, constricting and shutting off any more of my reasons to avoid Lexie's books, and her passing. The books called to me, and revived my desire to be inspired.

I spent the next few months rediscovering and reminiscing. My fondness for expression reinvigorated by the strength of Walt Whitman, the wind-through-the-trees imagery of Robert Frost. It was as if I had never grown and she had never faded, as if we were both still sitting on her bed, taken away from our mutual ills and individual laments by the feathered brightness of wisdom and emotion, creativity and mystery.

Lexie, lovely beyond compare, continues to inspire me, because of who she is, not who she was. She lives on inside of me, eternal and inexhaustible. Her presence in my life opened an infinite door... I step through it every day. As I write, I transform into something better, someone improved, a man inspired. Bathed in warm light, the internal aching chill of clanging metal doors and grating wind chimes of sharpened keys fades away; I breathe, deeply, eternally, and feel alive again, remembering this light has touched my face before. Just Lexie and I, laying on her pink bedspread, astonished at how lovely life is—how good it is to be alive.

Please visit the contest archives at pen.org/prison-writing for the full piece.

Honorable Mention, Drama

Tiny General
BENJAMIN FRANDSEN

FADE IN

MARCUS TIPTON

He's black, 12 years old, slender and well-dressed. His bearing and demeanor seem unnaturally serious. An extreme intelligence shines through his eyes with unnerving force. His small frame makes his mid-sized drone seem much larger.

DAVENPORT Now let's hear from Garfield High's youngest student, freshman Marcus Tipton. What have you got for us?

Gesturing to the drone, Marcus speaks quickly, almost robotically.

MARCUS I hybridized a Pixel 2 smartphone's high-res digital camera, a satellite zoom, and a drone with fully articulating grasping arms.

INT. OLD FOUR-DOOR SEDAN - NIGHT

Up front, bobbing his head to the RAP MUSIC playing on the car stereo, sits his brother RASHEED (17)-friendly, awkward, autistic. Their lovely mother, TARIQA (30s), frowns at her youngest son in the rearview mirror.

TARIQA What did I tell you about playing on that thing while we're driving, young man? Give it here.

THE OPPOSITE LANE ON THE SAME HIGHWAY

A gleaming new Dodge Challenger rockets towards the Tipton's like a bat out of hell. The driver, TYBERIUS WALKER (30s), grins, But his smile never reaches his eyes-cold eyes. He swerves around an 18-wheeler into oncoming traffic...

The Tipton's vehicle CRUNCHES roof-first into the ground, rolls twice, SHATTERING THE WINDOWS, and comes to a GRINDING stop, right-side up. Rasheed lies unconscious, his head bleeding. Tariqa, motionless, doesn't stir when Marcus prods her bloody side.

Finally she opens her eyes and looks from Rasheed to Marcus.

TARIQA (barely audible) You take care of your brother. You always were the strong one.

Her eyes close for the last time. Marcus's lips quiver, but he doesn't cry.

INT. TIPTON HOUSE - TARIQA'S WAKE - DAY

TAMMY (saccharine-sweet) Marcus, don't you look handsome in your little suit.

She frowns at his blank look. It's me, your Aunt Tammy. Yo' momma's half-sister? I'm gon' be staying with you and Rasheed awhile.

INT. TIPTON HOME - NIGHT

Bboyfriend T-BONE (30s) sits lazily in the couch, a crack pipe held loosely in his lap. She automatically slides into the seat next to him and takes his crack pipe.

TAMMY Where the lighter at?

Marcus rolls his eyes, pulling out his smartphone. Rasheed's full attention is focused on the TV screen as he plays the new Halo X-Box game, so he doesn't notice the lighter on the coffee table next to him. T-Bone abruptly boxes Rasheed's ear, hard.

MARCUS (icily) I told you that if you touched him, you were gone. That was the second time. Pack your things.

T-Bone lurches to his feet and raises his hand as if to backhand the boy, but Marcus holds up his phone to display a video. T-Bone pauses mid-strike.

INSERT - DRONE VIDEO FOOTAGE

BACK TO SCENE

T-BONE I will beat the bark off yo' little Erkel ass. Gimme that damn phone!

MARCUS Too late for that. I emailed that to your parole officer an hour ago. Only question now is whether you want to take this little head start I'm giving you and get the hell out now, or wait until they come scoop your "retarded ass" up.

KNOCK! KNOCK! KNOCK!

PAROLE OFFICER (O.S.) Come on out, T-Bone! I know you're in there!

T-Bone releases Marcus, runs out the back door—and right into the waiting arms of a patrol officer.

T-BONE Oh you gone see me again, you little son of a bitch!

TAMMY (sotto) Things 'bout to get real rough for you 'round here.

MARCUS If they do, you won't be here to see it.

Marcus pulls up something on his smartphone and shows Tammy.

MONTAGE - CLEANING UP THE CRACK HOUSE

—A UPS driver hauling several large boxes including two 52-inch flat-screen monitors into a clean house.

As his older brother plays a VIDEO GAME on one mounted screen in the living room/command center, Marcus studies the split-screen images of their house seen from the "eyes" of their outdoor security cameras.

Marcus counts out what's left of their depleted stack of cash. Glancing at the game Rasheed's playing, one where he's flying a military helicopter over enemy territory, Marcus grins mischievously.

MARCUS We ate into our stack of chips with all this, bro. We need to make some money. I'm going to need your help.

Rasheed PAUSES his game and looks at his little brother curiously. When he speaks, it's slow, deliberate, modulated.

RASHEED How does Marky need Rasheed's help?

The younger boy tilts his head conspiratorially toward the monitor Rasheed's using to play the game.

MARCUS How'd you like to fly a mission for real?

Please visit the contest archives at pen.org/prison-writing for the full piece.

Honorable Mention, Drama

Outcasts
MIKE PHILLIPS

Dear Mike,

How are you doing my loving husband? I hope you're okay and you have a pleasant day there always. I hope you are in good health condition.

I miss you very, very much and I love you very, very much. From the moment you were arrested I didn't have good sleep and I can't even eat till now and still in shock for what happened. I never speak this will happen. I cried when I wrote in this email. You're always in my mind every minute, every day. I worry about your situation and your food to eat inside the jail. I hope they have vegetarian food there for you. I miss you so much.

I answer your phone call every time you call me, but my phone cannot accept collect calls even I press answer. I'm still shocked even right now there is no day that I did not cry. I'm still in trauma, depression and stress. I never speak this will happen. I don't have no idea what's going on.

CHARACTERS

MIKE - a 65-year-old inmate of German lineage. He has no arrest record, is innocent of all charges. He is a writer, singer, and filmmaker. His health is rapidly deteriorating in jail.

ARCHIE - Mike's a 37-year-old husband, a Filipino immigrant. His life was threatened after Mike's arrest and he was convinced to return to Manila where his life is in extreme danger.

MILLIE - Mike's mother, 86-year-old, German/Slavic. A strong woman who always fought for her son. A bit hunched over from age and a hard life.

DON - Mike's father, 85-year-old, battered by life.

JAMES - A ghost of a murdered man. Bloody head and clothes.

Ray - The jail psychologist. 60-year-old. Authentic.

Joe - Mike's grandfather. Don's father. Serial rapist/pedophile.

Dark stage. Spotlight shines on Mike, a 65-year-old inmate dressed in orange. He is thin but in good shape, looks 40 rather than 65. Salt and pepper hair.

MIKE

My mother's family couldn't have cared less if you lived or died... my father's family wanted you dead. This is my legacy. Both of my parents were the best children of each of their families. They were good people. That's probably why they fell in love. They weren't perfect, but they did their best at parenting. I never doubted they loved me. But having grown up in such cold families I wonder where they learned to love. It's an argument for nature more than nurture. Yet, with Grandpa Joe's penchant for raping his children and grandchildren, can we support that argument? My father spent his entire life trying to get his parents to love him. They never did.

SITTING IN SPOTLIGHT, Archie, age 37, sick, homeless, disheveled, emaciated, weak, clothes dirty, unwashed. Sitting, crying. Alone in Manila.

ARCHIE

Where are you, my husband? Where are you, Mike? I'm lonely for you. You are my only family. I have no one. I love you. (crying.)

DIFFERENT SPOTLIGHT, Millie, age 86, hunched, wearing an old bathrobe and slippers.

MILLIE

Dammit, where's that dog hiding? Wally?

Where are you? Behind the couch?

Another SPOTLIGHT, Don, age 85, bent over from arthritis. Life has beaten him.

DON

My son. In jail on a murder charge. I told him he was too good to too many people and it would get him in trouble.

DARK STAGE, MIKE in spotlight, shirtless. Thin.

MIKE

My son, Archie. I call him my son as a joke. He is half my age but we fell in love and married. He is my best friend. My heart, soul, mind and body yearn for him. But he is 7,000 miles away.

My first partner, Bill, was a handsome man. Imagine Tom Selleck but even better looking. He is a Special Education teacher. We were together sixteen years. Then a younger guy convinced him I was no longer worthwhile and he dumped me, broke my heart. Nearly destroyed me. Everyone had seen us as the ideal relationship.

Then I met Mark. I didn't think I could get a better relationship than I had with Bill, but Mark and I were even better suited spiritually and politically. We became domestic partners. We traveled the world. Unexpectedly, after ten years, he developed a mid-life crisis and ran away. Took him eighteen months to make the break, but he disappeared. I tracked him down. He teaches high school math in Bangkok.

I think I had a nervous breakdown from that loss. It's all a painful blur, but I lived in San Francisco. I love the city like I love a person, so I maintained. I did fine being alone. Eleven years later, I'm "okay." I'm always busy, I never get bored. I didn't date after Mark left. I didn't date and I didn't crave sex. I met men, but they didn't reach the standard of Mark—or even Bill—so I remained single. There were some men who made it obvious they wanted me, even

said so, but I couldn't begin a relationship that could not be maintained. Why do that? Why lead someone on?

Out of the blue, I met an online penpal from overseas. His name was Archie. We had a lot in common, but he was in the Philippines, a place I had zero desire to visit, so I expected we would just remain pen pals. Over time we grew closer. Eventually we began Skyping. He was cute, handsome even. He was kind and sweet. So I decided to try to get him a work visa.

IN SPOTLIGHT, Ray. A therapist in the County Jail system. 60 years old. Grey hair. Glasses.

RAY

I recall the first time I saw Mike during his first week of incarceration, scared. Obviously he had never been arrested before, not for anything. Shaking like a small, frightened dog. Six months later he has come out of the fear. He is righteously angry.

ANOTHER SPOTLIGHT, James. Late 60's? Balding, comb over.

JAMES

I'm scared. Very scared. Two months ago I was doing well then last month I began losing all energy. Now the doctor says I have lung cancer. Stage four. How does that come on so fast? I go to my doctor every six months! How did they not catch that sooner? I don't have many people to rely on. I told my family, but they live too far away. I'm telling my friends, but I don't have many. When I told Mike, he said he would do everything he could to support me. Will he?

SPOTLIGHT, Mike dressed with shorts again. Speaking with his father, Don, on the phone in another spotlight.

MIKE

I need all the help I can get.

DON

I don't know what to do.

MIKE

I miss mother. She would fight tooth and nail for me. I have to tell you something. At my age I can't start over. If I lose all my belongings I will become a ghost, you will never hear from me again. You will never see me again. Your son will be gone forever. I. need. help.

(Silence on the phones. Mike hangs up.)

One Day Later. BOTH SPOTLIGHTS.

DON

Your niece will go to your house and put everything into storage.

SPOTLIGHT, Millie.

MILLIE

I would fight for my children like a lion. Well, maybe not my daughter, she's an asshole, hurt me. Treated me like crap. I raised them both to be good people. My Mikey, he turned out perfect, never caused me any trouble. His sister? A thief, a whore, probably did drugs. How did children from the same family turn out so different? It wasn't my fault. She got the bad genes. But I would fight like a lion for my son. You think he's a murderer? Come over here I'll slap your head off your shoulders.

SPOTLIGHT, RAY.

RAY

I've been a therapist for 40 years. You see the guilty and innocent, and between experience and schooling you can read people. Mike couldn't hurt anyone if he wanted to. He's suffering all the syndromes of a man in jail shock. "The eyes are windows to the soul?" I look into his eyes each week. He's worried about me being in danger with real criminals. Mike is just a man who was in the wrong place at the wrong time.

A JAIL CELL, BLEAK, MIKE on a chair

MIKE

The immigration lawyer said Archie did not have enough college education to get a work visa. My heart sank. But before I left her office she asked if I had emotional feelings for him. She said to come back if it ever developed into love, she also did fiancé visas. A month more of Skyping and I was back in her office.

I had to visit Archie twice to apply for the fiancé visa. He had no money so I went to Manila both times. I did not like Manila. 12 million people, too hot and humid for me, and the poverty was painful to see, worse than the U.S., worse than Guatemala or Thailand. The more I fell in love with Archie, the happier I was to be rescuing this wonderful man from a sure death. I did not like Manila, but I loved Archie.

SPOTLIGHT. ARCHIE, dressed and clean.

ARCHIE

After father and mother died I was alone. I had no one and was homeless. Just me and my dog. I was threatened by people in town, so I decide to go to Manila to take school. I cried as I left town. I had to leave dog behind. I lost mother, father, and dog. Dog watch me leave. He was confused.

I get to Manila and apply with caregiving school. Bank loan helped me with school, rent of small Room, little food. I use friend's computer to write emails. I want work visa to go to English speaking country. My mother told me as she died to look for someone to love me. She didn't know I am a gay. I pray to God very hard to meet a man to love me. Mike is only man who answered my bello e-mail. He is handsome but I don't think he will like me. He writes me once a week and then twice a week. Then we Skype every week and then once a day. I like him. I beg him to help me get work visa. Then he tells me he will visit me and likes me very much. I am very happy. He asks me if I love him. He is so good to me. I think I do love him.

SPOTLIGHT on James, covered in blood.

JAMES

Last thing I remember is I fell asleep sitting up on the couch. I have insomnia, so falling asleep any time is a blessing. I hear sounds from behind me. I am groggy. Sounds from the kitchen? What time is it? Seems like night. Is the caregiver here? I left the apartment door unlatched. Suddenly my head hurts, a voice I don't recognize says, "Where's your money, asshole? " Are my hearing aids in? I feel my head hurt again and slide off the couch. Blood drips in my eyes. I see a man but don't know if I know him. Blurry vision, voice unfamiliar, he jumps over couch. My head hurts again. I reach out to push him. Do I scratch him? I yell, "Stop hitting me!" and he hits me again. "Where's your money, fag ?" he screams. I crawl to my bed, onto the bed, he pulls me off. "I'll show you for marrying him, fucker! He should be marrying me!" I'm on the floor, he hits my head again and again. I'm so weak, I hurt so bad. How do they say it in movie scripts? "Fade to black"?

(Fade to black)

FLASHBACK 2016. MANILA. Mike and Archie in a car. They are dressed nicely, Archie driving him to airport.

MIKE
I go back to San Francisco now to have the lawyer submit our fiancé visa paperwork. We'll have you in the U.S. within 8 months. (Archie pulls car to curb. He sobs so hard he cannot see to drive.)

ARCHIE
(Sobbing uncontrollably. Deep sobs of anguish.) Thank you. Thank you. I'll miss you.

I love you. (Very deep, pained sobs.)

MIKE
Archie, being apart will be hard but it isn't forever. We will speak every day on Skype and Facebook and emails. As soon as the visa passes we will get you to America and we will marry. I love you. I will marry you. As soon as possible.

(Mike faces audience)

It was at that moment I knew made the right choice.

Honorable Mention, Drama

Never 2 Late
JOHN BENJAMIN

Act 1, Scene 1

Fade in: immediately see a five-stair stoop with a young African-American male sitting on them. He looks up and down the sidewalk as if waiting for someone. A well-dressed young man in designer clothes, casual, in his late teens, early twenties. Pulls phone out and dials in number:

RELL

How you feeling today?..I miss you too... Yeah, I'm waiting for Ki now, (Looks up and down the sidewalk again, then leans back on side of stoop so that his back is to stage right)

As soon as I get off you know I'm all yours...

Ki appears from stage right and walks up on Rell as his back is turned and listens to conversation.

RELL

What movie you want to watch tonight?... I'm thinking the

Notebook...

Ki frowns and starts to laugh quietly.

> RELL

That movie always gets to me, so you know it's only right if you shed a tear or two.

> KI

(Clears throat) Amm.

> RELL

(Quickly turns around) Which I don't want you doing tonight, so we're watching Jurassic World, alright! See you when I get home.

(Look at Ki suspiciously and turns head to give a kiss on the phone quickly than hangs up)

Why you always sneaking up on somebody?

(Does special handshake with Ki)

> KI

(starts laughing) You whipped you know that.

> RELL

No, no, I just like to spend time with my lady.

> KI

'My lady'?, what is this, Mid-evil times?

> RELL

See, that's what's wrong with you now, Ki. You need to learn how to talk and treat a female.

> KI

Don't try to justify being whipped.

> RELL

Listen, a brother that looks as good as me, there's no reason to be.

KI

Looks as good as you, my man: you so ugly when you look in the mirror your reflection ducks.

RELL

How you gon' talk about me? When you were a baby, your mother only got morning sickness 'til after you was born.

KI

(Both laugh and Ri shakes head as if he approves) You got me, you get me. What happened with that roommate situation. (Takes out cigarette)

RELL

Aww man Ki, first of all it was a female renting the two rooms out.

KI

Don't tell me you said something crazy to mess it up.

RELL

Nah. Listen, I told her about us and how we both have jobs, you have a car and how we'll just be good roommates. No loud music, we're clean, things of that nature.

KI

So what happened?

RELL

She said only one of us could move in, because she wants a male and female roomate.

KI

So did you take it.

RELL

How you gon ask me that. If we don't find nothing together then we'll wait til we do.

KI

So if you can get a place right now without me, dirt cheap, you not getting it.

RELL

No. We're a team, you know that. We been unseparable since we were five, if I get it, we got it, and nothing coming between that.

KI

Can't do nothing but respect that.(lights cigarette)

RELL

Besides, in a crib with two women, you know I'm not gon' have no type of win in that environment.

KI

(Chuckles) True, that's exactly why God created men before woman, he ain't want no type of advice.

Both laugh and do special handshake.

RELL

I'm a steal that one.

OLD MAN JOE (OMJ)

(walks out front door on top of stoop) Don't you boys start that hurting and hollering You both see my window open, and this about my time to take a nap. Now let me get a cigarette.

RELL

C'mon old man Joe, how you gen come out here a try to regulate.

OMJ

Regulate! What you want me to take action! Mess around and make a movie out of you two. Now where's Old Man Joe's Cigarette.

KI

(Chuckles) You lucky you known us since we been Kids. (Pulls cigarette out) Here.

RELL

We would make you an example.

OMJ

Don't threaten me with a good time! (Takes cigarette and lights it)

Now why you beys ain't at work? Don't tell me you out in these streets being dumb, trying to make a quick buck

KI

Now you know we don't dabble in that type of activity old man Joe. We just chilling before we go to work.

OMJ

You better not! Even though you two had your parent upbringing, you both got some of Old Man Joe's teachings in you. (Starts to walk down street)

RELL

I thought you was about to take a nap, where you going?

OMJ

Obviously Old Man Joe need some cigarettes, so by the time I get back hopefully you two be at work and Old Man Joe can take his nap.

(Searching pocket for something and drops a piece of paper on ground)

Shoot! (Reaching down to pick it up, but back goes out) Ooh my back! (Stands up straight)

RELL

You know you old when your back goes out more than you.

OMJ

Oh we get all the jokes today huh, with your belly button looking head

Rell looks stunned.

KI

(laughs and gets piece of paper) Barefoot Moscato, you don't drink wine old man Joe.

OMJ

(Snatches paper) Only when old man Joe got a date.

RELL

Oh yeah! I hope it ain't with Ms. Gladice.

OMJ

I'll see you boys later and stay out of trouble.

OMJ starts to walk off Stage left.

RELL

It is Ms. Gladice! Oh man, old man Joe you not that old! Her on the other hand, she so old she probably DJ'd for the Boston Tea Party.

All three laugh.

KI

She probably was a waitress at the last supper.

Both laugh harder and do special handshake. Old Man Joe looks back shaking his head laughing and gestures hand as to fan off the boys.

RELL & KI

Love is love.

OMJ

Love is love. Yeah, yeah.

Mailman appears stage right and walks up behind them.

MEL

Who you two ranking on now?

KI

Old Man Joe crazy ass.

RELL

A yo Mel, did you know Ms. Gladice and him have a date tonight?

MEL

Ms. Gladice! She so old she was in school when history class was called current events. (All three laugh) She so old she knew Burger King when he was a prince. (All three laugh extremely harder)

She so old she might pass away before the date tonight.

RELLE & KI

(Stop laughing immediately) Whoa, whoa whoa.

KI

God forbid.

RELL

Too far Mel, too far.

MEL

My fault.

Ki's phone rings.

KI

Hello.

Ki's expression gets serious. Rell and Mel in background talking, but they cannot be heard.

KI

What you want? Because we don't have nothing to talk about... Diapers! Look, I'm on my way to work, I don't got the time.

RELL

(Give Mel dap to leave) Who's that?

KI

(Gives Mel dap) Vivian.

RELL

Oh, that's the home girl! Hey Viv.

KI

(Pushing Rell back) If I knew better I'd do better, whats that mean?

RELL

I think that's quite self-explanatory

KI

(attention to Rell) C'mon bro.

RELL

Alright, alright.

KI

Listen, how many times I got to tell you, your on your own. I been told you what to do!... You gon' take my money now. I'll see you in court then!... Yeah, yeah, whatever.

Ki hangs up, starts to breathe heavy, and swings at air.

RELL

(looks around) What's happening right now?

KI

That chick be pissing me off bro.

RELL

Better to be pissed off than pissed on.

Ki looks angrily at Rell.

RELL

All jokes aside though. You had a rider, a smart fine wifey, What happened between you two?

KI

Tss, as you can see, all we do is argue.

RELL

I see that, but that tell me nothing. Now let me in Ki, what's going on with you two?

KI

It's just with her I see how women see men like bank accounts: without a lot of money they don't generate much interest.

RELL

(Takes a second to think) But, she was with you when you was broker... You know I keep it 100 with you Ki, I think you wild'n! You two used to be the hood's Jay-Z and Beyonce. You was winning with her, not to mention that's your baby mother man.

KI

And money hungry. As soon as I started getting my money up, she want to all of a sudden have a baby.

RELL

Well it's not like you two were practicing celibacy.

KI

Nah man, it's how it happened. As soon as I get this job, my car, and looking for a new apartment, she want to tell me she pregnant.

RELL

It got to be more than that.

KI

Oh it is. Check it, I sit her down and had a talk about having kids and I told her I wasn't ready.

RELL

That's understandable.

KI

But it's like, that went in one ear and out the other. I feel like she just disregarded what I wanted and just went with her own plan. If she really care about me she wouldn've had a baby.

RELL

You serious Ki! How you think babies are born? What you just
slipped and fell? Don't let your family be one of those broken family
statistics. You know you love that girl, plus you and I both know she
not one of them type of girls to trap someone like that.

KI

I don't want to be one of them statistics, that's why I told her to get
an abortion.

RELL

Are you crazy?? I'm glad she didn't, even though ya ain't plan to
have a kid it's here... I can't believe you ain't tell me this?

Both don't say anything for a few seconds.

RELL

Is it a boy or a girl?

KI

Boy... You think I'm in the wrong?

RELL

Without a doubt.

KI

You think she'll take me back?

RELL

Of course... Maybe... Probably not. But you have to work hard to
earn something or someone and even harder to keep them, so just
put in that overtime.

KI

(Shakes head, approving what Rell saids) I ain't gon stunt my B.M.
was official, and I do want to see what lil man look like.

RELL

Listen Ki, a woman who loves, comforts and serves. A man who loves, protect and provide. You like a brother to me bro. Go get you lady beck and take care of your son before it's too late Ki. I get you.

Ki and Rell do special handshake.

> RELL

You know I need parts of that Godfather role.

Attention shifts behind Ki to two African-American males sprinting past stoop and throwing a bookbag full of money.

> KI

I know that's not a bag of money.

> RELL

(Picks up bag and looks inside) Oh they wildn'...

Both look at each other.

> RELL

That means the police not far behind.

Both look in opposite directions down sidewalk.

> POLICE

(Gun in hand while running up to Ki and Rell) Stop right there! Drop the bag and put your hands on your head.

> RELL

Listen officer, the two perps you're looking for aren't us, they just throw this at us. I don't know how you missed them.

> POLICE

Wearing the exact thing you two are wearing right? Cut the shit and put your hands on your head.

Rell and Ki frown with thinking expressions on face.

> KI

The only thing we really had in common was they were black and so are we.

POLICE

Not gonna ask you two again. Put your hands on your head and turn around.

Rell throws bookbag. The Police point gun directly at him now.

RELL

We tryna be respectful.

KI

A yo chill, we gon be straight, you know this a block watch neighborhood, and somebody will vouch for us, we been on this stoop for like thirty minutes. (puts hands on head and turns to ground)

RELL

(Looks at Ki then the cop, and obeys) I hope you're right.

Police runs up to Ki and puts his knees in his inner knees to get Ki on his knees aggressively.

RELL

C'mon Sir, that's unnecessary.

Police quickly points gun back at Rell.

KI

Could of just told me to kneel down.

POLICE

Shut your mouth and keep your hands on your head.

RELL

Can you please get your gun out my face?

KI

Sir, we're both unarmed and we're not even a threat.

POLICE

(Calls in situation on radio) Suspects being contained on Winchester and Highland from the 10-16, requesting backup.

RELL

If you want me to stay like this till back up come I got chu. Can you get that gun out my face though?

KI

Stay cool.

RELL

How can I with this gun in my face.

POLICE

Shut up boy!

RELL

(Takes hands off head and uses them for expression while talking) Ki, you hear this crap. Sir, we're respecting you, respect us.

POLICE

(Yells) Put your hand back on your head and kneel down.

RELL

Sir, I'm a comply Just...

KI

(Shakes hands in aggravation) Just do it.

POLICE

(Starts to back up and points gun at Ki still yelling) Stop the sudden movements. (Gun back at Rell) And I'm tired of you boy, get on the ground now!

RELL

(Still using hands) I can hear you, just calm down.

POLICE

(Still backing up) Stop moving your hands.

KI

Stop moving.

POLICE

Do what I say boy.

KI

Just kneel and freeze.

RELL

(Throws hands up) Alri...

POLICE

Gun!

Police fires gun, and and Rell drops.

KI

(In disbelief) Nah, nah man. (Starts to cry and crawls to where Rell is) Nah, c'mon bro get up, get up bro.

Dispatcher comes on, and you hear how they caught perps with ink on hands. Police calls for paramedics.

KI

We gon' be late for work bro, get up.

OMJ

(Rushes to Ki and kneels next to him) Aww man Ki, what happened?

KI

(Sobbing) C'mon bro we got to go to work. I'll call Viv, that's my word. You got to get up cause you the Godfather. Please bro, just get up.

OMJ

(Grabs Ki and starts to get up with him and hugs him while giving Police a look of disappointment and disgust) C'mon Ki .

KI

We got to go to work Joe, we got to go..

OMJ

(Embraces Ki) I know son, I know.

Paramedics come and get Rell's body and Police walk with them offstage.

KI

I'm a get that pig back Joe!

OMJ

So you can end up in jail and not go to Rell's funeral? Use your head ki! I know who he was to you and what he meant to you. (Pushes Ki away from body but still holds him) Listen to me. Men control the action, the action should never control the man. You hear me? I know he was like a brother to you, but the only way out is through, and what we're gon' do is be strong and get through this alright?

Ki shakes head slowly and looks away.

OMJ

Time heals all wounds Ki.

KI

The thing with that is they may not heal properly.

OMJ

What's the ultimate measure of a man?

KI

What?

OMJ

What's the ultimate measure of a man?

KI

It's not where he stands in moments of comfort and convenience, but where he stands at times of challenge and controversy.

OMJ

That's right! And what we gon do?

KI

Stand tall.

OMJ

(Shakes head in approval and embraces him again) Let get out of here so they can clean this scene up

Both walk off stage arm on shoulders.

Fade out.

Scene 2

Fade in: Ki walks on stage scrolling through phone and sits on stoop. Inhales and exhales deeply and then dials a number.

KI

You still need them diapers ?... No wait, don't hang up. I'm not trying to be funny... I know and I'm sorry... Look I know I ain't been there for you or our son since you told me you were pregnant, but I'm calling you for your forgiveness and to ask you if I can come see you two... You're right, but... (Starts to get choked up) Rell died today, and all he wanted to do was go to work, go home, and spend time with his ... (Thinks about it) with his lady. Believe it or not I thought about you all today, and seeing Rell laid out on the sidewalk like he was, just made me think how everyday not promised to us... (Takes phone from ear and wipes eyes) If my heart could talk it be easier for me to express how I really feel about you, but I still have a lot of love for you. (Starts to get excited) I can be there in about fifteen minutes… Alright, I'll see you in a few… Hold up, hold up. Whats my son's name?... I like that (Hangs up phone, stands up, and starts to walk off) Kaleef.

Fade out.

I hope that readers can digest my work with intent and appreciate my writing without falling victim to the tendency to tokenize or romanticize the "real prison experience." If there's any beauty in the language I put into my work, I hope that the focus can be placed on that beauty, rather than some stereotypical benchmark of "rawness" or "realness." The people in my work, including myself, are real human beings who endure real consequences for their actions; I hope readers will focus on that.

In the end, I hope my work makes readers think. That's all I can ask for.

—Justin Rovillos Monson
2017 Honorable Mention in Poetry,
PEN America Prison Writing Awards and
2018 PEN America Writing for Justice Fellow

Acknowledgments

This anthology is made possible only because of the strong community that surrounds and buoys our small but mighty team of two. Very first on the list to thank: our dedicated PEN America Prison Writing Committee who contributed the time, and emotional and physical energy necessary to pore through over 1,000 entries... in order to shape the book in your hands.

Thank you to those who made this book visually sing: Tamara Santibañez for both the path that led us to our contributing artists, and for offering up a gorgeous illustration—and the freedom to experiment it into what you see today. Her original is a stark and striking masterpiece, included in the front of this book. Thank you to the contributing artists for dynamic visual responses to our writer's work, clearly created with much intention, thought and care. Wow!

Thank you to the following PEN America Prison Writing Program mentors who let us borrow their sharp editorial skills in creation of the Honorable Mention excerpts of all award-winning work: Allison Alter, Carlie Hoffman, Kim Rogers, Vincent Corsaro, Gary Winter, Billy McIntyre, Jennifer Keishin Armstrong, Morgan Peacock, Karen Stefano, Sarah Penner, Rangi McNeil, Cassie Robbins, Ariana Bacle, Christine Hope Davis, Sam J. Miller, and Helena Smith.

Thank you to our Spring and Summer 2019 interns: Lisa Nishimura, Giselle Robledo, Anjali Emsellem, Eleanor Mammen and Sarai Hertz-Velazquez, who supported our program in a vast number of ways including, but not limited to the rote work of transcription, answering letters, filing contest entries—in addition to the big picture creative work of curating writer's "sets" for presentation during our Break Out movement, and interviewing writers for the PEN America blog.

Thank you to literary superstars T Kira Madden, Nana Kwame Adjei-Brenyah, Kyle Swenson, Mitchell S. Jackson, and Tongo Eisen-Martin for your fantastic blurbs. Because one cannot jump on and search the Internet for these names in prison, we've included the bios on the next page. We hope our writers feel boosted by their genuine interest and support. These folks are the real deal.

Thank you to all of our tremendous colleagues at PEN America, and special gratitude to our communications team: Juliann Nelson, PEN America's Web Editor, for making sure the pieces in this book are all available, and beautifully displayed, on our website; Stephen Fee, Director of Communications for supporting this project full force; Hannah Lee for expert social media guidance. And of course, to, Dru Menaker, Chief Operating Officer and Suzanne Nossel, Chief Executive Officer, for engaged, responsive leadership, and enthusiastic support of our program.

Thank you to our program funders and the individual donors and PEN America members who have earmarked contributions for our Prison Writing Program—you continue to make all of this possible. We simply could not do it without you.

And finally, we know from our own experience that it takes a whole lot of guts and courage to risk rejection when submitting for publication. Thank you to all the writers who send work to our contest. Thank you for allowing us the opportunity to step into the worlds you live in, and create on the page. Please keep submitting to us—and everywhere.

Who Blurbed This Book?

T Kira Madden is a lesbian APIA writer, photographer, and amateur magician living in New York City. She holds an MFA in creative writing from Sarah Lawrence College and an BA in design and literature from Parsons School of Design and Eugene Lang College. She is the founding Editor-in-chief of *No Tokens*, a magazine of literature and art, and is a 2017 NYSCA/NYFA Artist Fellow in nonfiction literature from the New York Foundation for the Arts. She has received fellowships from The MacDowell Colony, Hedgebrook, Tin House, DISQUIET, Summer Literary Seminars, and Yaddo, where she was selected for the 2017 Linda Collins Endowed Residency Award. She facilitates writing workshops for homeless and formerly incarcerated individuals and currently teaches at Sarah Lawrence College. Her debut memoir, *LONG LIVE THE TRIBE OF FATHERLESS GIRLS*, is available now. There is no period in her name.

Nana Kwame Adjei-Brenyah is the New York Times-bestselling author of *Friday Black*. Originally from Spring Valley, New York, he graduated from SUNY Albany and went on to receive his MFA from Syracuse University. His work has appeared or is forthcoming from numerous publications, including the New York Times Book Review, Esquire, Literary Hub, the Paris Review, Guernica, and Longreads. He was selected by Colson Whitehead as one of the National Book Foundation's "5 Under 35" honorees, is the winner of the prestigious $75,000 PEN/Jean Stein Book Award, and a finalist for the National Book Critics Circle's John Leonard Award for Best First Book and the Aspen Words Literary Prize.

Kyle Swenson is a reporter with The Washington Post's Morning Mix team. Prior to joining The Post in 2017, he covered South Florida for the New Times Broward-Palm Beach. His reporting on the criminal justice system and features have won several national awards, including the Sigma Delta Chi award from the Society of Professional Journalists and the Salute to Excellence Award from the National Association of Black Journalists. In 2015 he was a finalist for the Livingston Award for Young Journalists. His work has appeared in The Village Voice, The New Republic, and Longreads. A graduate of Kenyon College, he lives in Washington, D.C. *Good Kids, Bad City* is his first book, which tells the true story of the longest wrongful imprisonment in the United States to end in exoneration.

Mitchell S. Jackson's debut novel *The Residue Years* received wide critical praise. Jackson is the winner of a Whiting Award. His novel also won The Ernest J. Gaines Prize for Literary Excellence and was a finalist for The Center for Fiction Flaherty-Dunnan First Novel Prize, the PEN / Hemingway Award for Debut Fiction, and the Hurston / Wright Legacy Award. Jackson's honors include fellowships from the Cullman Center of the New York Public Library, the Lannan Foundation, the Ford Foundation, TED, NYFA (New York Foundation for the Arts), and The Center for Fiction. His writing has appeared in The New Yorker, Harpers, The New York Times Book Review, The Paris Review, The Guardian, Tin House, and elsewhere. His nonfiction book *Survival Math: Notes on an All-American Family* was recently published by Scribner. He is a Clinical Associate Professor of writing in Liberal Studies at New York University. Jackson was a 2018 inaugural PEN America Writing For Justice Fellow.

Tongo Eisen-Martin was born in San Francisco and earned his MA at Columbia University. He is the author of *someone's dead already* (Bootstrap Press, 2015), nominated for a California Book Award; and *Heaven Is All Goodbyes* (City Lights, 2017), which received a 2018 American Book Award, a 2018 California Book Award, was named a 2018 National California Booksellers Association Poetry Book of the Year, and was shortlisted for the 2018 Griffin International Poetry Prize. Eisen-Martin is also an educator and organizer whose work centers on issues of mass incarceration, extrajudicial killings of Black people, and human rights. He has taught at detention centers around the country and at the Institute for Research in African-American Studies at Columbia University. He lives in San Francisco.

Does it ever occur to me that the summary rejection with which my work is customarily received could be based upon its lack of merit rather than a discriminatory act of classist passive aggression?

No. It doesn't.

—Sean Dunne
Featured writer, 2019 PEN America/Poetry Project
BREAKOUT: A Movement

What Incarcerated Writers Want the Literary Community to Understand

What do you want us to know about the experience of being a writer in prison? Or being a writer outside of prison (the label, the stigma, the space)? Or both!

ZEKE CALIGIURI: I would say that writing is hard, and it can be so much harder when it comes from a place where it isn't supported by anybody. There isn't always typing opportunities, and so much of the editing and revision processes are excruciating. And honestly, people who run these places don't care if you are a writer or the greatest living artist on earth—they want the facility to run as simply as it can be. Individualism is stifled. Then there is the censorship. Anything can be deemed threatening. So, we become so protective of our art, and so much of our energy goes into protecting our ability to create. It's a whole second level of survival that we are constantly aware of; one, our own, two, our work.

SEAN THOMAS DUNNE: I want you to know that I absolutely fucking hate being a "prison writer." It makes my allergies flare up just thinking about it. It's like every editor's desk at every literary journal, publishing house, annual writing contest, and school newspaper is just inundated with submissions from "prison writers", or something. And these cheezedick motherfuckers are really driving down the value on my shit. I try to decorate my envelopes in a spunky way so as to distract my recipients from the bullshit parental advisory label that the cockknocker who reads the outgoing mail stamps on there. But nothing's doing. It's come to the point where I'm certain that "STATE PRISON GENERATED

MAIL" is interpreted as "THIRD RATE TRIPE FROM A PILE OF HUMAN GARBAGE". Oh, man. You gotta know how much I hate it.

Does it ever occur to me that the summary rejection with which my work is customarily received could be based upon its lack of merit rather than a discriminatory act of classist passive aggression? No. It doesn't.

Now, as pertains to the second part of your question about being a writer outside of prison, I will admit to this much: I've spent 1/4th of my life in prison, it's true. But what the fuck was I doing the rest of the time? If I was so worried about the horrid connotation of being a prison writer then I shouldnt've spent the other 3/4th's shooting up and masturbating in a bush.

JUSTIN ROVILLOS MONSON: Seeking out thoughtful, honest feedback on my work has often felt impossible, let alone submitting anything for publication. This lack of accessibility to a viable literary community has made me feel perpetually alone, like it's all pointless. On the other hand, if you put in the work, you can have some successes. The danger comes, I think, when you feed into the idea of being a "prison writer." I've heard quite a few times of the romanticized notion of the poet, working with fire and fury, alone at their desk. Though probably unconscious, I think this notion is often attributed to the poet in prison, by both the poet and the outside literary community. This image isn't necessarily a bad thing—it can be what drives a poet to write and what generates a hunger for their work—but I think it can also lead to false ideas of what it means to grow and thrive as an artist. Of course there are exceptions, but I really believe that writers—like any other human beings—need community more than they do a sense of personal legend. The writer in prison faces a paradoxical dilemma, one of working against both carceral isolation, and romantic arrogance; of both attempting to transcend the "prison writer" label, and taking advantage of the literary community's hunger for marginalized voices.

B. BATCHELOR: I am lucky enough to be part of an amazing writing community with the Stillwater Writers Collective (a large group of inmate writers who support each other through writing) and the Minnesota Prison Writing Workshop. I think that I am much more fortunate than many incarcerated writers around the country who are not afforded this opportunity. From the very beginning I have been nurtured and supported and given the creative space to spill myself on the page. It is tough dealing with the internal issues of the prison environment (the noise, the constant hassle, the inherent negativity, etc.), and in the past we have not been given much of a chance in the publishing community, whether with literary journals or independent/major publishers. The landscape for us has completely changed. I feel that the "inside" and "outside" writing communities have blurred the stigmatized lines and there is growing support to have our voices heard.

CHARLES NORMAN: Prison officials in Tallahassee (headquarters) frequently republish my work on their websites and even Facebook. Many guards tell me they enjoy my writings, and learn from them. Others, who have the chain gang mentality that all prisoners are scum, subhumans who don't know their places, who need to be taught lessons, are the ones I avoid, since there is no room for positive dialogues with such closed, hateful (mostly ignorant) minds. I have experienced retaliation from prison staff for my writing, and been locked up in solitary confinement for my work. A corrupt mailroom supervisor had me locked up over a poem I wrote (a PEN prizewinner), and when she brought my legal mail to my cell, she told the escorting officer, "He's a fucking poet." I won a federal retaliation lawsuit against her, and she lost her job for lying, filing false disciplinary reports, and stealing postage stamps, but that didn't give me back the time I spent in solitary.

RAHSAAN THOMAS: Being in prison allows me the time and space to focus on a writing career. I don't have to worry about lousy pay for beginning writers or crushing bills that may have forced me to pursue a career other than this one I love so much. However, without email access (which we don't have at San Quentin State Prison in California) or a full time secretary on the outside, it's difficult to submit work to most organizations because they only accept stories sent through Submittable, which requires going online. The days of handwriting or typing up stories and mailing to a magazine editor are nearly at an end. Unless the prison system makes some changes, writers who are incarcerated may soon be heard from very seldom.

In what ways can you envision a lasting connection with literary community outside the walls? From your perspective, what can we do to be more inclusive, or to help shift the narrative?

JUSTIN ROVILLOS MONSON: The most exciting part of receiving the Writing for Justice Fellowship from PEN America was being the possibility of being a part of—and less apart from—the literary community. I sincerely hope, as time goes on, I can further feel not only that I belong, but that I am making meaningful contributions of work to that community and tradition, beyond being recognized and appreciated mostly—or solely—for my contributions as a "prison writer." I think, if you want to change the narrative surrounding writers in prison, programs and organizational mechanisms and practices need to continue to push us to write beyond prison. By that I don't mean the content shouldn't be centered in the institutions that have shaped our lives so tangibly, but that the bar should be set high enough to demand quality work over the possible tokenized inclusion of marginalized voices, and the resources made available to us should reflect that demand. The literary community as a whole should continue to ask tough questions about its role in responsibly cultivating and giving audience to the voices of incarcerated writers. Some of these questions might be: How can we make it easier to find and submit to our platforms? What can we do to match up the work of incarcerated writers to publications that will appreciate the individual works? And what steps can we take to push incarcerated writers beyond the "prison writer" label and into the mainstream literary fray, while still honoring the stories and content that come from the prison experience?

B. BATCHELOR: Personally, I would love to be able to have access to more writers/poets on a one-on-one level, creating possible relationships with my contemporaries as if I were an MFA candidate making meaningful connections along the way. One of my favorite things to do when I receive a new poetry book is to find the acknowledgments page and read all the names the poet thanks for their friendship and partnership in creating the poems in the book.

RAHSAAN THOMAS: If possible, create a Submittable assistance program where incarcerated writers who sign up are notified of publishing opportunities and are assisted with editing and sending in their work.

LOUISE K WAAKAA'IGAN (AKA KAROL HOUSE): There needs to be more conversation with prison staff and administration for them to see the value and importance of writing opportunities, classes, computer time, support groups. I am fortunate to have a strong supportive network within the facility here, yet I know not every writer on the inside has this.

ZEKE CALIGIURI: The simplest way to be more inclusive of our community is to read our work. Don't necessarily segregate us from the rest of the literary landscape as a specific body with specific politics and culture. The incarcerated are just as nuanced and different from each other as artists and personalities as the spectrum that exists in free literary circles.

CHARLES NORMAN: Encouraging those in the literary community to write letters or emails to prisoners, if nothing else, to say they enjoyed that person's work, or offer encouragement, could be meaningful to someone locked in a cell with no other human contacts. By making the prisoners' addresses available, and encouraging citizens to write them could change someone's life. I've had an email address for over 18 years, a website and blog for over 11 years [that my wife runs], and that has been life changing for me. I've received comments from readers in 100 countries over the years. A 25-year old single mother in South Africa wrote that she'd been reading my blogs for three years, that life was hard in her country, but if I could survive and live a positive life under my circumstances, she could, too. That makes a lot of suffering worthwhile. Give the prison writers some positive publicity, send them copies they may use for their freedom efforts.

SEAN J. WHITE: The incarcerated are famished for connection. Outside of prison people go to where the literary community congregates—readings, bookstores, workshops, et cetera. We have little of that here, and that which we do is typically brought from the outside. I feel it necessary to say that although some in prison have less than ideal intent, most have a genuine desire to have a reciprocal relationship (I use that word in the broadest sense) with those who communicate and connect with them. Additionally, gatekeeping (in the literal and metaphorical sense) creates issues. Prison staff deny access at times to those wishing to say, run a workshop, and impose numerous restrictions on those they do let in. From the literary community gatekeeping occurs because of the sheer volume of requests—insufficient money, insufficient time. For anything to succeed requires grassroots development. That is, if a non-incarcerated writer "adopts" one incarcerated writer into his or her circle, or a bookstore "adopts" twenty five to fifty incarcerated writers, eventually the majority receive the connection they need and desire as enough people and venues participate. The problems always develop because the desire/need for connection by the incarcerated exceeds the capacity of any one person, organization, or venue.

I have three suggestions to make a more lasting connection between incarcerated writers and the literary community. First, bring more workshops and reading to jails and prisons. The poet Bruce Dethlefsen visited New Lisbon Correctional Institution several times while I resided there. Unfortunately, he is one man, and there are over a hundred prisons, correctional centers, and county jails in Wisconsin alone. Second, a regular compilation of news and notes for and about incarcerated writers. Finally, I would suggest something akin to PEN America's mentorship program, though on a grander scale. Unfortunately, anonymity costs money. However, in a system operated by, say, a bookstore, such correspondents could pay for postage and use the address of the venue that a person might visit regularly any way. In those cases where a prisoner has access to Corrlinks (an electronic messaging service—growing more frequent in application) or something similar, a postcard could be sent with a name and email address. The likelihood of potential crimes perpetrated against a correspondent seem minimal. Writing a cross-country prisoner would diminish that further, as most blue-collar crimes involve drugs, and what drug-addled mind drives hundreds of miles to burglarize a home (Truman Capote's book offering an outlier).

SEAN THOMAS DUNNE: I hope my work will be received with the unyielding enthusiasm of a fucking Beatlemaniac at Shea Stadium in 1965. I want so many people to be screaming in ecstacy that you can't even hear what the fuck I'm saying. I want to be invited to spend the night at your house and I wanna drink your beers and smoke your bud and I want to be d.j. and master of ceremonies all night long for the meaningful experience that we're gonna have. I want to be written letters of love and hope precipitated not by some bourgeoise charity agenda but predicated instead by the value of my personality and talent. I wanna take L.S.D. with you. I wanna ride bikes with you. I wanna Facetime with you. I wanna lend myself to care about your problems, and when shit goes sour between you and your old man I wanna be the alkaline base that uncurdles your funk. I wanna talk to you about punk rock. Fuck, man. I shoulda put that first. Aw Christ, I been thinkin' about this one a long time!

Great Heavens to Mergatroid! I wanna listen to new bands with you and cut and paste collages and write zine's with you on your bedroom floor. I wanna hold your hair back when you puke, girly. Wanna buy you a corn dog, girl. You gotta check out my double kickflips and my pressure flips. Fakie pressure flips. Pressure flips for days, girl. And seahorses fuheva.

We could totally watch all the horror movies I've missed these last five years I've been upstate. Aw, man. You don't even know. This one time I sat there and watched all the Halloween's with this beautiful gothic girl named Crystal. I sat through ten hours of Michael Meyers, and don't get me wrong, I was fully into it cause I love horror movies, and plus we had just narrowly escaped the iniquitous obsession of methamphetamine possession and we ate and slept finally, and her dad came by and took us to rent movies, so we were just smoking long bud and feeling the serenity of 1980's horror creep into the synaptic knobs of our overused dopamine receptors, and just doing it grande. But inasmuch as I had a lifetime lasting episode of joy to reflect upon and look back on in the real life horror movie that would ultimately envelop the rest of my life, I also had a monumentally miserable experience 'cause I wanted her so bad. But Crystal just didn't feel that way about me. One by one. Halloween 1,2,3,4,5? The whole time flailing in the dichotomy of joy and abject torment as she sat there in her tiny boxer shorts on her futon, beside me. It was awful.

But maybe it won't be like that with you. Maybe this time you'll just look at me the way I always wished she had, and we'll go and put bottles of dish soap in the fountain at city hall and we'll start an acoustic punk band and we'll hang out at Tompkins Square and Battery Park and when the cold weather comes, and when the rain comes, and when the dope runs out, and when the cops come and take us away and we wake up on the holding cell floor and we have to kick, at least we won't be alone. That is what I hope to accomplish when I put my motherfucking pen to page.

Maybe it's hard for you to imagine this, but I have tears in my eves cause no one has ever thought to ask me that question. So, I would like to yield the floor to the little blue eyed boy inside me, staring out the window, waitin' for mom to come home at three am: the answer to your question is I just want to be your friend.

Made in the USA
Middletown, DE
18 November 2020

24345413R00161